Sarah Bartlett is a trained ast
reader with many celebrity
frequently broadcasts on TV
capacity. She is the author of the best-selling
Feng Shui for Lovers and *The Five Keys of Feng Shui*.
She lives near Cambridge.

Also by Sarah Bartlett

Feng Shui for Lovers
The Five Keys of Feng Shui

火
土
金
水
木

Feng Shui
for
Entertaining

SARAH
BARTLETT

VISTA

To Faith

This edition first published in Great Britain in 1999 by Vista
An imprint of Orion Books Ltd
Orion House, 5 Upper St Martin's Lane
London WC2H 9EA

A CIP catalogue record for this book
is available from the British Library

ISBN 0575 603372

Contents

Introduction

Be not forgetful to entertain strangers,
for thereby some have entertained angels unawares.
Hebrews, New Testament

HOW TO USE THIS BOOK

Feng Shui For Entertaining is a simple guide to creating harmonious and beneficial energy for any social occasion, whether a formal dinner party, a business lunch or a soirée for friends. By using energizers, changing colour schemes or simply knowing the kinds of energy your guests respond to, you can ensure the occasion goes smoothly and successfully.

The book looks at all aspects of entertainment for adult parties including romantic dinners and business lunches. You can find out each guest's personality profile and work out where the best place is for them to sit at the table. And you will discover how to use the simplest of energizers in any contemporary Western interior.

BASIC PRINCIPLES OF FENG SHUI

The art of Feng Shui is based on a system of harmonizing the environment. Basically, 'Feng' means wind, and 'Shui' means water. The ancient Chinese believed that man, living creatures, the world and everything in it were connected by a flow of universal energy. What the Wind and Water did was tell you what kind of energy was running through the mountains, the landscape and ultimately your home.

The wind is known as Yang, active dynamic energy, and water as Yin, passive, receptive energy. The simple balancing of these two forces of nature became Feng Shui. Even contemporary scientists agree that the whole universe vibrates and inter-connects via some unknown force or energy. In the art of Feng Shui this energy is known as ch'i.

This energy is a powerful force, and it must be used for the good of everyone, not just for personal gain, although it can be used to empower and improve your business deals, possibilities for financial improvement or simply to ensure your party goes smoothly. Remember that what goes around comes around!

This book shows you how to use some of the basic principles of this exceptionally intricate system. There are many books on the subject, and there are many confusions about which partic-ular school of thought to follow. My own philosophy is to try out the simplest approach first. Feng Shui is only a part of the larger system of Chinese astrology. Therefore, if you know about the five elemental types and the energies that correspond to them, you will immediately have enough information to start.

Knowing what kind of people you have invited, their personalities, and the energies that are also already present in the venue are all you need to work with.

The magic of Feng Shui is that the enhancements and remedies you use establish a certain kind of energy flow, so that the ch'i is able to move in harmony with the occasion, and ultimately will encourage your guests to be part of it and enjoy themselves.

Energy flow round dinner table

CREATING THE MOOD

Whatever mood you want to create, Feng Shui remedies and balancers can help. Even if you are called to a mysterious location for a secret romantic dinner, or have to go out to a restaurant with friends, there are tips and ideas for every occasion. But harmony begins at home, and if you are embarking on a party or occasion that demands forethought, then you can prepare yourself and your home to ensure a good outcome.

For the purposes of ease and accessibility, this book avoids trying to combine a multitude of seemingly contradictory directions. The art of successful entertaining is to use the techniques of Feng Shui that are the most practical. Only when you've been working with Feng Shui for a long time can you really get to grips with all the different energies you have to harmonize. Simplicity means basics. Basics mean that the essence of Feng Shui lies in the ability to be at one with your environment, your guests, and with yourself.

WHAT IS YIN AND YANG?

In Chapter One you will find a chart and table to look up your animal sign and your birth element. This also tells you whether you are naturally Yin (passive) or Yang (dynamic) energy.

The Chinese are very aware that the types of food we eat are important depending on whether we are Yin or Yang types. Yin people are, on the whole, quiet, introverted and often appear laid-back and unexcitable. Yang people are dynamic, aggressive and appear determined and confident. However, there are certain states in which you may be overcompensating for your energy expression, such as when you are stressed, restless, uneasy or head over heals in love. This is why your Yin/Yang energy will fluctuate. A naturally Yin person may appear very

Yang and therefore needs to be careful about balancing their internal energy levels with the outer and external world. Furthermore, the food we eat is either Yin or Yang, and there are also foods which are neutral, or balanced between both.

Yin food is cooling and transforming, Yang food is hot and inspiring. Even if you know the kind of temperament and personalities of your guests, it is important to ensure that the food you provide is a good balance of Yin, Yang, and neutral foods, to ensure harmony. There are sections throughout the book which give guidelines for Yin and Yang food, drink and balancers.

CHAPTER ONE

The Animals, the Elements, Feng Shui and the Bagua

Knowing your guests' energy type is very useful for planning any party or occasion. If you don't know or can't find out their year of birth, then use the simple method of numerology on page 8.

The Chinese use a lunar calendar, and therefore the dates of the changeover for each year varies. In the following pages is a chart of elements and animals from 1900 to 2003 which also tells you whether your energy is either Yin or Yang.

THE ANIMALS

Your animal sign represents the inner qualities of your personality, and although not always obvious to outsiders, is an important part of your identity. It is very like your star sign in Western astrology. This will help to give you more insight into your guests, especially if they are strangers, or new to your business affairs.

THE ELEMENTS

This is your outer energy expression. It is the way you move through space, it is the way you respond and react to circumstances and events. There are five elements, Fire, Earth, Metal, Water and Wood. You will find throughout this book that the balance of these elements in relation to your home and yourself is the main key to successful entertaining.

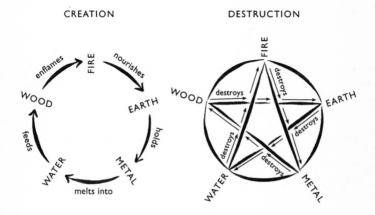

Diagram of elements in flow showing creative/destructive cycles

YIN AND YANG

Whether you are Yin or Yang determines the way you channel the energy expression of your animal and element signs.

CHART OF ANIMAL AND ELEMENT SIGNS

31 Jan 1900 *to* 18 Feb 1901	Rat	Metal	Yang
19 Feb 1901 *to* 7 Feb 1902	Ox	Metal	Yin
8 Feb 1902 *to* 28 Jan 1903	Tiger	Water	Yang
29 Jan 1903 *to* 15 Feb 1904	Rabbit	Water	Yin
16 Feb 1904 *to* 3 Feb 1905	Dragon	Wood	Yang
4 Feb 1905 *to* 24 Jan 1906	Snake	Wood	Yin
25 Jan 1906 *to* 12 Feb 1907	Horse	Fire	Yang
13 Feb 1907 *to* 1 Feb 1908	Sheep	Fire	Yin
2 Feb 1908 *to* 21 Jan 1909	Monkey	Earth	Yang
22 Jan 1909 *to* 9 Feb 1910	Rooster	Earth	Yin
10 Feb 1910 *to* 29 Jan 1911	Dog	Metal	Yang
30 Jan 1911 *to* 17 Feb 1912	Pig	Metal	Yin
18 Feb 1912 *to* 5 Feb 1913	Rat	Water	Yang
6 Feb 1913 *to* 25 Jan 1914	Ox	Water	Yin
26 Jan 1914 *to* 13 Feb 1915	Tiger	Wood	Yang
14 Feb 1915 *to* 3 Feb 1916	Rabbit	Wood	Yin
4 Feb 1916 *to* 22 Jan 1917	Dragon	Fire	Yang
23 Jan 1917 *to* 10 Feb 1918	Snake	Fire	Yin
11 Feb 1918 *to* 31 Jan 1919	Horse	Earth	Yang
1 Feb 1919 *to* 19 Feb 1920	Sheep	Earth	Yin
20 Feb 1920 *to* 7 Feb 1921	Monkey	Metal	Yang
8 Feb 1921 *to* 27 Jan 1922	Rooster	Metal	Yin
28 Jan 1922 *to* 15 Feb 1923	Dog	Water	Yang
16 Feb 1923 *to* 4 Feb 1924	Pig	Water	Yin
5 Feb 1924 *to* 23 Jan 1925	Rat	Wood	Yang
24 Jan 1925 *to* 12 Feb 1926	Ox	Wood	Yin
13 Feb 1926 *to* 1 Feb 1927	Tiger	Fire	Yang
2 Feb 1927 *to* 22 Jan 1928	Rabbit	Fire	Yin
23 Jan 1928 *to* 9 Feb 1929	Dragon	Earth	Yang
10 Feb 1929 *to* 29 Jan 1930	Snake	Earth	Yin

30 Jan 1930 to 16 Feb 1931	Horse	Metal	Yang
17 Feb 1931 to 5 Feb 1932	Sheep	Metal	Yin
6 Feb 1932 to 25 Jan 1933	Monkey	Water	Yang
26 Jan 1933 to 13 Feb 1934	Rooster	Water	Yin
14 Feb 1934 to 3 Feb 1935	Dog	Wood	Yang
4 Feb 1935 to 23 Jan 1936	Pig	Wood	Yin
24 Jan 1936 to 10 Feb 1937	Rat	Fire	Yang
11 Feb 1937 to 30 Jan 1938	Ox	Fire	Yin
31 Jan 1938 to 18 Feb 1939	Tiger	Earth	Yang
19 Feb 1939 to 7 Feb 1940	Rabbit	Earth	Yin
8 Feb 1940 to 26 Jan 1941	Dragon	Metal	Yang
27 Jan 1941 to 14 Feb 1942	Snake	Metal	Yin
15 Feb 1942 to 4 Feb 1943	Horse	Water	Yang
5 Feb 1943 to 24 Jan 1944	Sheep	Water	Yin
25 Jan 1944 to 12 Feb 1945	Monkey	Wood	Yang
13 Feb 1945 to 1 Feb 1946	Rooster	Wood	Yin
2 Feb 1946 to 21 Jan 1947	Dog	Fire	Yang
22 Jan 1947 to 9 Feb 1948	Pig	Fire	Yin
10 Feb 1948 to 28 Jan 1949	Rat	Earth	Yang
29 Jan 1949 to 16 Feb 1950	Ox	Earth	Yin
17 Feb 1950 to 5 Feb 1951	Tiger	Metal	Yang
6 Feb 1951 to 26 Jan 1952	Rabbit	Metal	Yin
27 Jan 1952 to 13 Feb 1953	Dragon	Water	Yang
14 Feb 1953 to 2 Feb 1954	Snake	Water	Yin
3 Feb 1954 to 23 Jan 1955	Horse	Wood	Yang
24 Jan 1955 to 11 Feb 1956	Sheep	Wood	Yin
12 Feb 1956 to 30 Jan 1957	Monkey	Fire	Yang
31 Jan 1957 to 17 Feb 1958	Rooster	Fire	Yin
18 Feb 1958 to 7 Feb 1959	Dog	Earth	Yang
8 Feb 1959 to 27 Jan 1960	Pig	Earth	Yin
28 Jan 1960 to 14 Feb 1961	Rat	Metal	Yang
15 Feb 1961 to 4 Feb 1962	Ox	Metal	Yin

5 Feb 1962 to 24 Jan 1963	Tiger	Water	Yang
25 Jan 1963 to 12 Feb 1964	Rabbit	Water	Yin
13 Feb 1964 to 1 Feb 1965	Dragon	Wood	Yang
2 Feb 1965 to 20 Jan 1966	Snake	Wood	Yin
21 Jan 1966 to 8 Feb 1967	Horse	Fire	Yang
9 Feb 1967 to 29 Jan 1968	Sheep	Fire	Yin
30 Jan 1968 to 16 Feb 1969	Monkey	Earth	Yang
17 Feb 1969 to 5 Feb 1970	Rooster	Earth	Yin
6 Feb 1970 to 26 Jan 1971	Dog	Metal	Yang
27 Jan 1971 to 14 Feb 1972	Pig	Metal	Yin
15 Feb 1972 to 2 Feb 1973	Rat	Water	Yang
3 Feb 1973 to 22 Jan 1974	Ox	Water	Yin
23 Jan 1974 to 10 Feb 1975	Tiger	Wood	Yang
11 Feb 1975 to 30 Jan 1976	Rabbit	Wood	Yin
31 Jan 1976 to 17 Feb 1977	Dragon	Fire	Yang
18 Feb 1977 to 6 Feb 1978	Snake	Fire	Yin
7 Feb 1978 to 27 Jan 1979	Horse	Earth	Yang
28 Jan 1979 to 15 Feb 1980	Sheep	Earth	Yin
16 Feb 1980 to 4 Feb 1981	Monkey	Metal	Yang
5 Feb 1981 to 24 Jan 1982	Rooster	Metal	Yin
25 Jan 1982 to 12 Feb 1983	Dog	Water	Yang
13 Feb 1983 to 1 Feb 1984	Pig	Water	Yin
2 Feb 1984 to 19 Feb 1985	Rat	Wood	Yang
20 Feb 1985 to 8 Feb 1986	Ox	Wood	Yin
9 Feb 1986 to 28 Jan 1987	Tiger	Fire	Yang
29 Jan 1987 to 16 Feb 1988	Rabbit	Fire	Yin
17 Feb 1988 to 5 Feb 1989	Dragon	Earth	Yang
6 Feb 1989 to 26 Jan 1990	Snake	Earth	Yin
27 Jan 1990 to 14 Feb 1991	Horse	Metal	Yang
15 Feb 1991 to 3 Feb 1992	Sheep	Metal	Yin
4 Feb 1992 to 22 Jan 1993	Monkey	Water	Yang
23 Jan 1993 to 9 Feb 1994	Rooster	Water	Yin

10 Feb 1994 to 30 Jan 1995	Dog	Wood	Yang
31 Jan 1995 to 18 Feb 1996	Pig	Wood	Yin
19 Feb 1996 to 6 Feb 1997	Rat	Fire	Yang
7 Feb 1997 to 27 Jan 1998	Ox	Fire	Yin
28 Jan 1998 to 15 Feb 1999	Tiger	Earth	Yang
16 Feb 1999 to 4 Feb 2000	Rabbit	Earth	Yin
5 Feb 2000 to 23 Jan 2001	Dragon	Metal	Yang
24 Jan 2001 to 11 Feb 2002	Snake	Metal	Yin
12 Feb 2002 to 31 Jan 2003	Horse	Water	Yang
1 Feb 2003 to 21 Jan 2004	Sheep	Water	Yin

Use the animal and element signs information for any occasion, when there are fewer than eight people. You will find each chapter deals with different ways of using Feng Shui in more detail depending on what atmosphere you are trying to create.

If you have more than eight guests then the elements and energies will more than likely balance themselves out.

THE BAGUA

The other Feng Shui principle you need to draw on to balance your guests' and your own personal energy is a map of interior spaces called the Bagua.

Knowing how to use the Bagua, in a simple and practical way, will ensure also that the environment and your guests are in harmony. This is crucial.

The Bagua For Entertaining

The Bagua is a grid system of the invisible energies at work in your environment. Feng Shui practitioners use the Bagua map placed over your room, your house, and even your table, to see which areas of the Bagua correspond to which parts of the room. The Bagua will give you the key areas of the room or table where you need to place remedies and enhancements to reinforce your own energy. This is particularly useful when entertaining difficult guests, i.e. at a business lunch, or when you are unsure of your guests and their own inner energies. It also means you are bringing into alignment the harmony not only of yourself and your guests, but also the empty spaces and flow of ch'i in and around your home.

How To Use the Bagua

The Bagua is based on the magic number square as shown below. This square has mystical powers in the Chinese system. Whichever way you add up the lines the total comes to fifteen. In the West this number isn't particularly significant, but in the East it is considered magical and powerful. Each of the nine numbers corresponds to an invisible energy that exudes a certain quality. These invisible energies are everywhere, but by using the Bagua in a simple way you can locate specific areas of your home, dinner table or room, depending on the harmony, mood or energy level you are trying to achieve, without worrying about your guests' element or animal signs. This is useful for big occasions when you really don't want to weigh up the significance of every animal sign and elemental energy of thirty guests! A large number of people will usually ensure a good balance of elements. What needs reinforcing then is your own element, and sometimes the modification of the environment according to the Bagua.

Each of the nine numbers refers to a type of energy, and has a Chinese keyword traditionally associated with it. Because the essence of Western entertaining is different from the cultural and social traditions of the East (although of course we do eat Chinese food and enjoy the pleasures of Chinese philosophy, arts

*Magic
Number
Square*

4	9	2
3	5	7
8	1	6

*Magic square
becomes
the bagua*

WIND 4	FIRE 9	EARTH 2
THUNDER 3	CORE 5	LAKE 7
MOUNTAIN 8	WATER 1	HEAVEN 6

and literature), we have a Western heritage and a Western soul to go with it! We can't be truly Eastern, any more than the Eastern nations can be truly Western. Chinese traditions and etiquette are peppered with old patriarchal systems and values, although imbued with the balanced approach of the ancient Feng Shui arts. For entertaining purposes I have given modern interpretations to these classic Bagua symbols.

In each of the following chapters you will find different ways of using the Bagua depending on who are the guests, and what kind of entertainment you are planning.

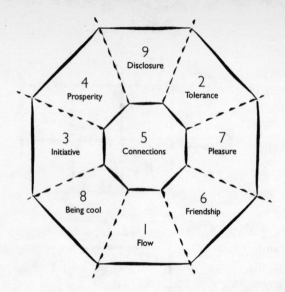

Diagram of entertaining Bagua

9 Disclosure
4 Prosperity
2 Tolerance
3 Initiative
5 Connections
7 Pleasure
8 Being cool
6 Friendship
1 Flow

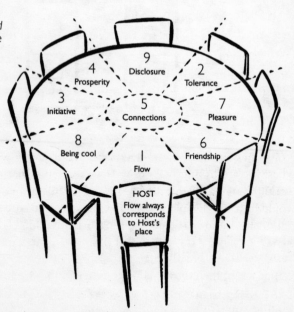

Diagram of Bagua aligned to round table

9 Disclosure
4 Prosperity
2 Tolerance
3 Initiative
5 Connections
7 Pleasure
8 Being cool
6 Friendship
1 Flow

HOST
Flow always corresponds to Host's place

Flow

WATER — Your journey forward and your sense of personal freedom. Enables you to plan your journey or new direction in life. Area of the Bagua for business ventures and deals, the area of the party or dinner table which corresponds to Water is where you can impress for maximum benefit. Always seat yourself as host in this position.

Tolerance

EARTH — How you receive others into your life and your heart. Receptivity. Also an area of the room or table to enhance to ensure you reap the benefits of hard work. Guests who only like the sound of their own voice can be placed in the seat corresponding to this area to ensure that they listen to others!

Initiative

THUNDER — Outside influences, those who are your superiors/parental involvement. How you have been shaped by your family/society. The vitality of your inheritance. The area of your dinner table or room that corresponds to advancement.

Prosperity

WIND — Often known as the 'money area' of your house. Promotes good luck and grace rather than merely wealth. It is where we are prosperous in ourselves as well as in the material world. The area of the dinner table that corresponds to Wind would be a suitable place for certain guests who may be beneficial to you in business.

Connections

UNITY — This is where the areas of the Bagua unite. Harmony here is essential. A key area of the house, room or table which is often overlooked. This is where all energies pass through —

a threshold to oneness. As this will always correspond to the centre of the table, there are important enhancements to be placed here depending on the occasion.

Friendship

HEAVEN — Unconditional friendship, support and sharing, between individuals and collectively. A useful area for business associations and promotion both in business and in other affairs. A useful area of the Bagua for big social occasions and large parties where you can't see the wood for the trees. Place your allies here!

Pleasure

LAKE — Intimate relationships and sexuality. Pleasure and sensuality are keywords here, there is a sense of the sun rising, the moment before release of the energy that creates new life. Romantic dinners and intimate feasts may benefit from enhancing this area of your home and bedroom. A good area of the Bagua to enhance for complete relaxation.

Being Cool

MOUNTAIN — This is an area for communication and inner wisdom. There is a sense of awareness of what you do not know, rather than what you do know. This is a crucial area for containment, and for conception of ideas. Balance is necessary here to encourage the individuality of each guest and yet avoid selfishness.

Disclosure

FIRE — Are you in tune with your objectives? Clarity and insight. An important area of the table or room to enhance for media and publicity, fame and any kind of creative accomplishment. But if you're trying to keep a secret avoid sitting in this area! If you *want* someone to spill the beans, get them to sit here.

Placing the Bagua

Make a copy of the Bagua diagram on a piece of tracing paper and then make a drawing of your room, home or dinner table. Line up the bottom edge of the Bagua with the wall that corresponds to the main door or entrance. The front door of your house or the main door through which you welcome your guests is very important, for this is where the flow of the ch'i starts. If using just a room, line it up with the doorway wall of the entertaining room. If you are placing it over a table, make sure that the bottom edge of the Bagua is placed in line with your seat as in the example below.

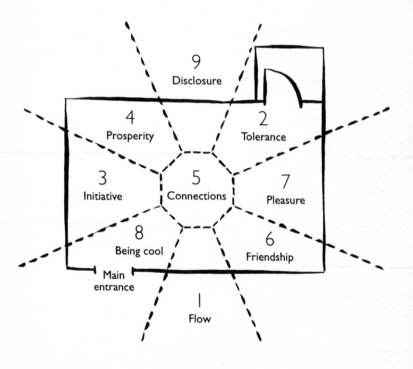

Placing the Bagua for your house

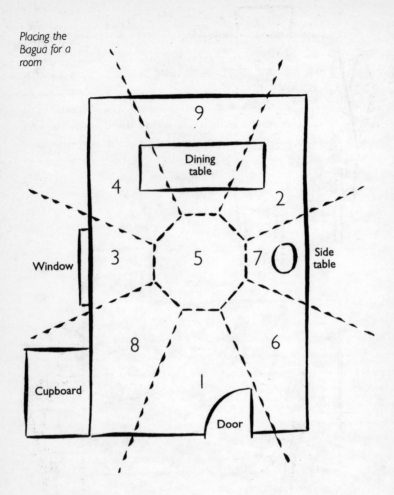

Placing the Bagua for a room

9

Dining table

4

2

3

5

7 O

Window

Side table

8

6

1

Cupboard

Door

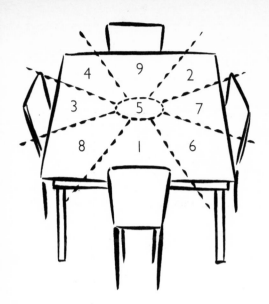

Placing the Bagua for a square table

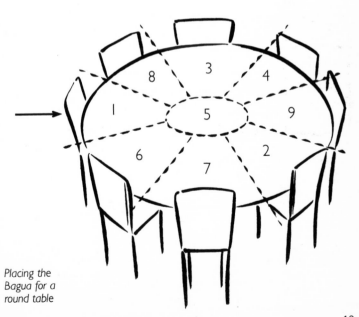

Placing the Bagua for a round table

19

THE HOUSE

The house itself also has its own energy balance depending on the direction it is facing in relation to the ch'i – the great universal energy that flows through everything. The direction of the house is determined by the direction of the ch'i as it flows into the house through your main front door – the door you open to your guests, the world and strangers. This is the most important entry zone of your home, and if you've just moved in it's worth aligning the natural energy of the house with that of your own, or your household.

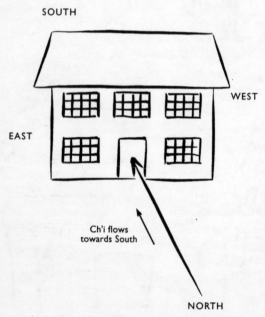

Principle direction of the house

Are You Compatible With Your Home?

The chances are your own birth element is not in harmony with your house. In this case you need to bring in some simple cures to align the balance of elements. Following are some suggestions. However, if you run through the list below and find your direction and your dominant element aren't mentioned, then you can assume they are harmonious and you're off to a good start.

If the dominant element of your family or household members is Fire and the direction of the ch'i entering your house is north:

Remedy – Place a red candle, a tall upright plant, or a piece of carnelian in the north side of your home.

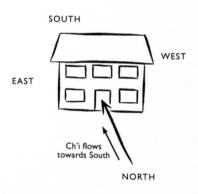

If the dominant element of your family or household is Water and the direction of the ch'i entering your house is either south or south-west:

Remedy – Place a piece of amber or lapis lazuli in the south, south-west area of your home. Alternatively place or hang an image or photo of moving water.

If the dominant element is Wood and the direction of the ch'i entering your house is west or south-west:

Remedy — Place malachite or green tourmaline in the west or south-west area of your home. If you can't get hold of these, use a piece of old gnarled wood or a wooden bird or paper sculpture.

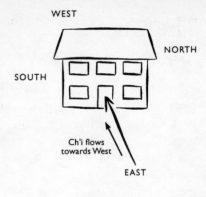

If the dominant element is Metal and the direction of the ch'i entering your house is east or south:

Remedy — Simply place some clear white quartz crystal in the east or south of your home. You can also use a metal wall sconce with a white candle, or place a metal container filled with old coins.

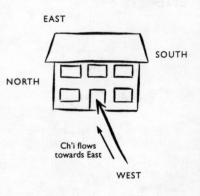

Now you are ready to turn to Chapter Two to discover more about your Feng Shui profile as a host, and that of your guests. There is also a compatibility chart on page 61 to check out the suitability of guests and/or combination of clients.

The Guests

HOW TO FIND OUT YOUR GUESTS' ENERGY FLOW

Before you start laying tables, placing crystals and moving the furniture, you need to know a bit about the people you have invited. As already mentioned, if you have more than eight or even a dozen people at any one gathering then the energy will be fairly balanced and it is only the atmosphere and the environment that need harmonizing.

If you can find out your guests' dates of birth then you are off to an excellent start. If you can't, or find it too difficult or embarrassing to ask, then there is a numerological solution. All you have to do is look them up in the chart on page 60 to find out their birth animal and element. The following section gives you a profile of how each element resonates and reacts to circumstances and events at a party, and what kind of energies guests with these elements will exude. Their animal signs provide a satirical and light-hearted guide to the pros and cons of their basic personality traits.

THE ELEMENTAL ANIMALS
– YOUR GUESTS

When faced with sheer indulgence, the delights of being entertained or amused, we often resort to the most primitive way of
behaving. Some of us stiffen our lips, tighten our buttocks and
hope we don't say or do anything socially unacceptable. Others
turn into wild animals of the forest, dancing manically after the
first few drinks have released them of their inhibitions and
hang-ups. In other words, being entertained can bring out our
best and our worst sides.

If you keep a sense of humour rather than become judge-
mental, then you may find your tolerance of your guests, or of
the other invitees, enables you to relax and enjoy yourself. You
don't have to be the life and soul of the party to entertain or be
entertained, but you do have to be wise.

This guide to the Elemental Animals will help you understand
the way your guests behave in a social environment, and later
you'll find useful Feng Shui enhancements and remedies for
dealing with the different types. Remember, whatever their
animal sign, it is their *element* that will dictate how these people
get on with others at parties. For example, if you look in the
chart on p. 54, you will see that a group of Fire animals will
circulate well with lots of Wood and Earth and they may find
Metal and Water hard work but decidedly stimulating!

THE PARTY 'ANIMALS'

Fire Energy Is Passionate

FIRE RAT

Either fun to have around or totally nerve-racking, depending on your own temperament. Unpredictable in their moods and behaviour, they can be awkward guests at business functions, especially if they are supposedly on your side of the deal! Fire Rats take advantage of any discussion and can turn it into a quarrel just for the fun of it. They are, however, great at public speaking and love dramatic, flamboyant dos and luxurious occasions. They are the kind people who always win raffles, and somehow manage to sit at the table next to the most important person – if it's not themselves! Invite them to extravaganzas and they'll be a tremendous asset.

FIRE OX

The dependable Fire Ox may be insensitive to others' feelings at parties, but their own are acutely vulnerable! These people tend to assume they know everything and can be irritatingly critical about the food, the drink and, worst of all, your other guests. Their honesty is impeccable, but usually their manners are the best. Fire Ox people of both sexes are conscious of how they appear and will turn up dressed exactly right for the occasion. Don't give them the chance to be unbearably smug at dinner parties. They can be extremely sarcastic and unappreciative of the cuisine which took you three days to prepare and cook. Do invite them to formal events, don't invite them over to exchange small-talk with your long-lost family.

FIRE TIGER

Being thoroughly unrestrained in everything they do, Fire Tigers are apt to roar through your party without a thought for anyone else's fun except their own. Mind you, they are glamorous, dramatic and full of enthusiasm as they tear up the drive with a host of friends tagging behind. Extremely popular, they'll rarely need amusing, more likely they'll amuse everyone else at the dinner table. However, they need action and fun, so don't expect them to hang around long for intellectual conversation, or long-drawn-out speeches. These people are restless provocateurs, and if you manage to invite any of them to your party you'll ensure dynamic energy abounds. However, they may roar off again down the drive with all your other guests in tow after they suggest a moonlight swim in the nearest lake! Do invite them to big fun events, don't invite them to formal dinners.

FIRE RABBIT

These guests are either loved or hated. They demand to be the centre of attention and really do believe that they can have everything their own way. This, of course, may conflict with your own plans for the evening. You may be forced to flatter and praise these guests all night to the neglect of the others. To give these guests a sense of achievement, suggest they lay the table if they arrive early (and they often do), polish the glasses (if it's a banquet you can keep them amused for hours) or do all those fiddly jobs with bits of cheese, smoked salmon or skinning chicken breasts. However, if faced with any kind of confrontation these rabbits will run, so don't invite them to deal-clinching lunches, but do invite them for their managerial qualities at press functions.

FIRE DRAGON

Don't underestimate Fire Dragons. They are dazzling and insist on being so. If your party is to be a quiet affair and not go much further than dinner-table chit chat, then don't invite a dragon, they might get over-heated and blast their way out of your home. Fire Dragons are impatient and need to feel they are special. They feel most comfortable at occasions when they can move quickly around the assembled company seeing who they can inspire with their rich imagination and creative genius. Don't invite them to pragmatic family discussions over a Sunday roast. Do invite them to masquerades, feasts and sumptuous entertainments!

FIRE SNAKE

Like other Fire animals the Snakes are no different. Out for a really dynamic and passionate time, they are hugely dramatic and yet terribly worried about their own needs. Fire Snakes love smaller gatherings, places where they are already popular or at least know the guests. Don't think because they aren't punctual they haven't any idea about the time. This is just to confuse you. Fire Snakes are cunning and can be extremely punctual. If they arrive late it's because there is a reason for them arriving just at a specific moment. Whatever you do, don't underestimate them. They will eat everything in sight, and charm everyone with their conversation and witty words. But behind that passionate and charismatic exterior lies a deadly and often ruthless mind. These Snakes mean business, and may have as many enemies in tow as they do friends, so watch out who you invite! Do invite them if you want an intriguing time, don't invite them to house-warmings.

FIRE HORSE

These people are volatile and optimistic. They are daring, love action and prefer dynamic fast-paced dinner parties and challenging business lunches. They're always ready to get on with the next course and often seem arrogant and self-centred, not passing the salt or offering to wash up. Yet their vanity and impulsive ways hide a deep insecurity and a desperate need to live up to their own high expectations of themselves. They are fun to have around at grand occasions and press receptions, but perhaps are too hasty, blunt, and impatient for laid-back soirees and intimate dinner parties where they are likely to upset those who don't understand their headstrong qualities.

FIRE SHEEP

Of all the Fire types Sheep are probably the most willing guests at your party. They prefer larger crowds where they can merge unobtrusively because they often worry about how they look or whether they are overdressed. Fire Sheep enjoy circulating and listening to the conversation of others and they make generous and lively companions. They are sought-after guests, though they can be mildly pedantic about who they spend their time with, preferring to be associated with wealth and elegance, rather than eccentricity or bohemianism. These people are better at larger parties because they prefer the solidarity of the masses rather than the vulnerability of being only one of four or six. Do invite them to banquets and large bashes, don't invite them to intimate, eccentric or bizarre cocktail parties.

FIRE MONKEY

These are the kind of guests who either bring a dynamic vitality to any occasion, or simply turn it into a fiasco. These are good-time monkeys. They're audacious and egotistic, and they'll demand to be centre stage, expecting everyone to take their passions as seriously and as vehemently as they do. You may find them holding court in the kitchen, but they are often the first on to the dance floor, or at the buffet table. They can be charming risk takers, and like the best champagne or the biggest piece of cake. They have no scruples: watch them climb over your furniture, rummage through the contents of your freezer for ice cream and always win at Twister. You may decide that next time you'd prefer a more tranquil and less inspirational occasion. Do invite for fun occasions, don't invite for quiet dinner parties.

FIRE ROOSTER

Independent in the extreme, these guests create a stir wherever they go. Eccentric yet extravagant they'll be loud, flashy and full of confidence. Keep them in reserve for difficult family parties where you can be sure their frank and enthusiastic teasing of everyone in sight will amuse them, at least. Sometimes known as the party dissidents, these guests get bored easily and may leave in dramatic fashion, only to return at the crack of dawn, just to remind everyone of their presence in true rooster style. Give them the best cuisine and the responsibility for opening the wine and they'll be stylish guests and good organizers to have around. Do invite them to possible boring occasions just for the fun of it, don't invite them if you are trying to impress.

FIRE DOG

These people are impulsive, jumpy and prone to drinking and eating as much as they possibly can. They are just as arrogant as the other Fire animals, but more able to carry off a kind of innocent charm, an almost `abandoned dog' look, when it suits them to get their way. Highly attractive, they bound around at parties kissing everyone, and often flirting with the host. Do invite them for fun celebrations, don't invite them for serious business.

FIRE PIG

These guests eat well, enjoy life to the full and are only happy when everyone around them is as cheerful as they are. They aren't fond of intellectualizing over the dinner table and would much rather get on with the pleasures of eating and drinking. These people love to be adored, and will take centre stage at your party without much encouragement, organizing games, mixing the punch while they finish the nuts, crisps and cheese biscuits so they can stroll into the kitchen for more. Do invite them for family occasions and big business events. don't invite them to intimate dinner parties.

Earth Energy Is Grounded

EARTH RAT

If you invite an Earth Rat into your home, you'll probably find them happiest in the kitchen. These people are quietly weighing up the practical advantages of how you've laid out the buffet, rather than sharing in the chat and gossip like other Rat types. However, they are not so keen on large social functions or business occasions, as they are actually quite scared of anything new. Don't try giving them the latest fad in Icelandic cuisine or squid wrapped in lettuce leaves. These are people who feel safe with the tried and tested. Just don't try to test them! Do invite them to formal dinners and in-house business lunches, don't invite them to large social parties unless they know everyone.

EARTH OX

You can usually rely on your Ox guests to help out and be the quiet, but efficient type in the kitchen. They prefer to help serve the drinks and wash up rather than be bright conversationalists or what they may think of as crashing bores. They exude a quiet impatience with the more dynamic guests, and need to be reminded that at the end of the party they can look forward to an extra portion of their favourite cheesecake. Earth Ox people are highly conscientious, so make the most of them at your party, give them plenty of tasks and don't try and palm them off with anyone you're trying to impress, because they actually have a tendency to think they know it all. Do invite them to informal gatherings, don't invite them to intellectual dinners.

EARTH TIGER

Earth Tigers are lucky and fascinating to have at any occasion. They enjoy and prefer formal, conventional parties and places and other guests who are sensible and civilized. Underneath their veneer of down-to-earth common sense these guests have a fiery need to provoke a reaction. They may start off politely shaking their head when you keep on offering the vol-au-vents, they may cover their glass with their hands when you come round with a top-up. But as the evening progresses you may find these guests become less worried about their party intake, and more frivolous as they think how they can make an impression. Great to have at barbecues and informal get-togethers, even dinner parties, but watch out at serious business lunches for a twist in these Tigers' tails!

EARTH RABBIT

These guests come out of their warrens and socialize frequently if given the chance but only if the atmosphere is elegant, the conversation civilized and the environment stylish and beautiful. They prefer dinner parties and quiet informality to huge, noisy discos or barbecues. They avoid the harshness of reality and aren't particularly fond of ruthless business meetings or parties where everyone seems to be having an affair with everyone else. They have a problem making up their minds and so you may find when you offer them a choice of cheese or pudding they'll retreat to the safety of the loo for half an hour, or more likely they'll go home to contemplate in more familiar surroundings where decisions are easy. Do invite them to formal lunches and dinners, don't invite them to noisy outdoor events.

EARTH DRAGON

Dragon guests are notorious for being unreliable. They are always in a rush to arrive, and then equally in a rush to go. However, the Earth Dragons are probably the more civilized of the Dragon family, able to make it at least halfway through the buffet lunch before they begin to twitch uncomfortably and glance at their watch. Their excuses are usually more sensible than the rest of their fellow Dragons, and they have a greater sense of responsibility. In their race to finish their food before anyone else, these guests are reasonable when eating cool or lukewarm food, but if given red-hot chillis or similarly yang fare, they can become much more controversial! Do invite them to quick business lunches, or informal suppers, don't invite them to long-drawn-out feasts or ten-course weddings!

EARTH SNAKE

Have you ever noticed those guests who sneak in the back door at parties and usually prop up the kitchen sink most of the evening, never having been near the frantic dancing in the sitting room, or the overcrowded hallway and loo? These are usually Earth Snakes, sensual and graceful, who seem to slip into your house and out again before you've even had time to check if they were invited. Hating crowds they'll coil in your kitchen or back room, or even in the garden, waiting for you to find them. However, they love small intimate occasions, especially if they know everyone in the room, and are very good at delighting everyone with their down-to-earth humour. Do invite them to small close friends' parties, and don't invite them to huge gatherings.

EARTH HORSE

Reliable people, who always turn up promptly and leave politely on time. Their behaviour is impeccable, but they have big appetites and also big prejudices. Don't get into an argument about the best way to cook souffles or bake bread with these guests as they will undoubtedly have been on a three-year course on the exact subject. However, they can be distracted easily with tasty appetizers and loads of aperitifs which will mellow their intolerance for other peoples' humour, which is never as funny as their own. Useful stallions and Arab mares at business lunches, but just heavy horses at fun dinner parties.

EARTH SHEEP

You can usually spot Earth Sheep guests by the way they seem so relaxed and laid-back. They seem neither to worry about the drink supply, nor attempt to flirt, tease or taunt. These are social people who don't have pushy egos, but won't take criticism either. If you try to talk at an Earth Sheep they'll usually back off quickly and retreat to the bathroom or the comfiest sofa. Their defence is the crowd, but if you do pick them out for verbal slaughter you'll meet a quite extraordinary resistance and retaliation will be swift. Do invite them to most informal and large social gatherings, don't invite them to family get-togethers.

EARTH MONKEY

Wily, wise and more intellectual than most, Earth Monkeys can turn any occasion into a highbrow affair with a twist. Their knowledge is unquestionable and their ability to get out of any difficult conversation with a double entendre or inventive speech make them excellent guests at business dealings. They prefer parties that are well organized, small and structured, but if the other guests aren't ready to listen to their extraordinary conversational antics, and the cuisine isn't terrific, your Monkey will sulk in a corner. Do invite them to impress and add gravitas to your business dealings, don't invite them to large gatherings where they may flounder without intellectual stimulus.

EARTH ROOSTER

More reliable than other Roosters, these guests will be ready to pass the vegetables, enjoy meals that are on time, and hosts who are immaculate both in timing and in cleanliness. If they notice a crumb on the table they're sure to clean it up before anyone else, and if your best Water Tiger friend spills red wine on the white cloth you may discover this Rooster already covering the area with salt and pointing out they have observed how this method always works over the many parties they have attended. They may also suggest how clumsiness can be avoided. These guests are acutely critical, cool, confident and insightful. Do invite them for their extraordinary, odd behaviour, but don't invite them to conventional parties or nail-biting deals.

EARTH DOG

These are excellent guests at business occasions because they can suss out anyone's motives with their persistent manner and inner wisdom. They prefer small dinner parties and soirées, and they'll eat very little compared to other Earth animals. However, you'll find them slipping into the kitchen later, ravenous for scraps and titbits. Like other Dogs, these guests are friendly and sociable, great to have at any occasion and are generally peaceable but ready to leap into action when required. Train them to wash up, and you'll have useful guests for life.

EARTH PIG

These people are reliable and have a great instinct for self-preservation. They are loyal friends and colleagues and prefer lavish food, intimate and laid-back dinner parties to formal dos. They can also be wild sensualists, and will make excellent guests for lengthy feasts. Their ability to be intuitive about others means they are useful at business functions. They make good head-hunters, and always know the right people to invite to someone else's party! However, because they are stubborn and often over-cautious they may lack the necessary verve to sustain all-night celebrations or to join in with the masses. But they'll always wash up. Do invite them to big dinners and banquets, don't invite them to all-night parties.

Metal Energy Is Progressive

METAL RAT

Loners at heart, these people are blessed with the ability to get on at any function, and feel that they are there for a purpose. Usually their own. They are very secretive, yet gregarious, ambitious, yet somehow nice about their objectives. Useful to have at business lunches, their charming magnetism will draw out of others the most highly guarded financial secrets. Like other Rats they enjoy being entertained, as long as they are in control of their space. Metal Rats prefer smaller gatherings to banquets and balls, but their charming and witty presence will ensure that the most difficult of parties will be a success, because if they are invited then they are motivated to make sure it succeeds. Do invite them to impress, don't invite them to large social gatherings, where their charisma is wasted.

METAL OX

These are people who invariably make their presence felt as soon as they enter the room. They are charismatic, powerful and can never be thwarted. If you invite Metal Oxen to your home, ensure you are ready for their rather serious and often demanding ways. They may contemplate the wine label long after most of the other guests have knocked back the first glass. They may ponder and prevaricate about which of the buffet dishes seems most appropriate to their current palate. However, these people won't let you down, will always arrive on time, and can be sure to protect you from gatecrashers. Their timing is immaculate, so they make great human clocks if you want a business lunch to be concluded by a certain time! Do invite them to business-deal lunches, don't invite them to frivolous suppers.

METAL TIGER

These are the kind of guests who'll stealthily creep in at the last minute and seem as if they've been there all night. If you want to liven the place up — say at a family gathering of aged aunts and assorted relatives you haven't seen for fifteen years — they'll be the first to shock and take a few risks. Given the opportunity, they'll be totally unrestrained in their drinking and eating. Free beer, wine and champagne will ensure that they stand near the bar or table for the best attacking position. They are shrewd and magnetic and can be depended on for getting more restrained guests to open up with their articulate but sometimes invasive conversational art. Do invite them to wine tastings or for their wit and insight, don't invite them to formal dinners with not much to drink.

METAL RABBIT

Like other Metal animals, Rabbits can be intensely intolerant of everyone else at the party, but also highly observant and complimentary if the quality of their surroundings and the feast before them are up to their extraordinary high expectations. These are critical and sometimes cold guests to have around. They are often loners, not looking for partners, but merely fascinated by how other people tick. They will be polite, immaculately dressed and hard to please. But their loyalty is to be cherished, and their integrity respected. They may frustrate you with their lack of compassion, but don't be fooled: underneath a cold and steely exterior lies a deeply emotional and artistic soul. Invite them to paint you a mural in your loo while everyone else is panicking about the buffet, and see what happens! Do invite to them fine and well-organized occasions, don't invite them to informal, noisy parties.

METAL DRAGON

Powerful guests who can drain your party spirit as quickly as you can produce it. Metal Dragons are ruthless and fierce in their convictions, so if you want heated discussions over the dinner table then invite them frequently! If you have a gentler time in mind, make sure they are happy to sit with less formidable guests. It's not that they are really any worse than anyone else, it's just if given half the chance they'll take over the show. However, they are excellent in a crisis and if your fridge has broken down they'll be the first to drive a hundred miles in search of a friendly restaurant to supply your ice. Do invite them to incisive business lunches and dinners, don't invite them to informal or light-hearted occasions.

METAL SNAKE

Metal guests will be either with you or against you, so take care. If they have come as friends and colleagues then they will be loyal and offer the highest support. If they are challenging business competitors or uninvited guests they can be intensely ruthless. Snakes of this type enjoy small intimate gatherings, where they can be mysterious and the centre of quiet attention. Although they say little they seem to organize the party rather than participate in it. Controlled and determined to succeed they make excellent speakers, brilliant strategists and the kind of person you want around if you need to impress strangers or make a speech. However, they will walk out of a party without a goodbye if they are feeling lonely and moody, which is often. Do invite them to small gatherings, don't invite them to barbecues and noisy dance parties.

METAL HORSE

If you want guests who break the rules, are innovative, wild, outspoken and glamorous in the extreme, then invite a few of these charismatic creatures. Avoid inviting a herd of them, however, or you'll end up with a stampede through your kitchen, and any serenity or formality is sure to be trampled on in seconds. These guests prefer big occasions, wild and out-rageous parties where they can make a lot of noise, generally look fabulous, much to the envy of everyone else, and then blaze off into the sunset without a thank you. Not to be recommended for faint hearts, but definitely worth inviting for their irresistible and innate sexiness. Do invite them to huge parties and press receptions, don't invite them to intimate soirees, or dainty tea-parties.

METAL SHEEP

Inviting these Sheep to your party or going to one where you know they are lurking can be an endurance test. These guests are contradictory creatures, loners who want to be in the crowd, determined and ambitious to compete, yet vulnerable and sensitive, beneath a rather showy and coarse facade. They may appear all mouth and not much else, but deep down they are insecure. Their loyalty, will-power and strength of purpose render them useful at business parties. Metal Sheep enjoy extravagant living and the beautiful things that go with it, so make sure your taste is impeccable, and that your other guests are prepared for their sometimes vulgar observations. Do invite them to glamorous events, don't invite them to informal, impromptu suppers.

METAL MONKEY

Like the other Metal animals Monkeys won't come to your party unless they have a reason, or an ulterior motive. They are ruthlessly self-controlled, and are bound to attract a group of ogling admirers around their vivacious chatter and non-stop wit and wisdom. These are Monkeys that are easily admired and just as easily loathed. Getting to know them is fraught with crossing every psychological boundary, so leave them to get to know you first, when you might have a chance of catching a glimpse of the sensitivity that hides behind these cool and constantly darting eyes. Great for impressing others, but not so great for relaxing your friends. Do invite them for business planning lunches, don't invite them for a quiet evening of drinks and Monopoly.

METAL ROOSTER

Great for analyzing everyone at the dinner table with their microscopic observations, yet awkward and often too intense about life, if all you want is light-hearted conversation and gossip. These guests have to be in control of your party, and in the most cheerful and glowing way they will usually achieve it. Watch out for the ones who don't look you in the eye, they are quietly sussing you out as they listen. They are loyal when they choose to be, as long as there is something in it for them. Stroke their egos, not their feathers, and you can be assured of success and reward. Do invite them to large crowded parties, don't invite them to light-hearted suppers.

METAL DOG

The lone-wolf types, guests who prefer the cool evening air to the bustle and sweat of the dance floor. They are hungry for power, so watch out if they put on enchanting social niceties: beneath this charm are cool people with very defensive natures. They really are quite lonely, and may wander into a party just to try and find out how sociable they can be. Excellent guests on your side for entertaining business competitors, and wonderfully charismatic if you want glamour and the smell of success. Metal Dogs are always good at everything they do, and being the perfect guest can be an absolute challenge, so they'll play the part well. Do invite them to formal dinner parties and for business completions, don't invite them to bustling barbecues or all-night parties.

METAL PIG

Make sure you have endless supplies of food and drink if you invite these guests as they have tremendous appetites. These people excel at getting to the top in the nicest possible way. They are ruthless at business parties, but they always seem to get away with their ferocious tenacity for winning, by slapping everyone else on the back and saying better luck next time. They prefer large informal occasions simply because they can avoid getting too intimate with anyone. Metal Pigs are as big on suspicion as they are on appetite so *do* invite them to large cocktail parties where they can impress, and *don't* invite them to spend an evening with close friends of yours they have never met.

Water Energy Is Restless

WATER RAT

Water Rats are usually frivolous, fun and gregarious, which makes them great party guests. They love romantic locations, elegant surroundings and charming conversation. They are communicators and enjoy the chit-chat of informal occasions and smaller formal dinners equally. They adapt, so they'll fit in with most occasions, ready to merge, change and listen. However, they can become bored too quickly with the same company if it doesn't stimulate them. They are also prone to not turning up when invited, and turning up when not! Keeping their hosts on their toes is their favourite trick. You'll often find them in your kitchen scrubbing potatoes, then five minutes later they'll have flirted with every member of the opposite sex in the room. *Do* invite them for light-hearted and informal parties, *don't* invite them to heavy business lunches or lengthy formal banquets.

WATER OX

These are the diplomats of the Water animals. Although they suffer from insecurity, they can allow themselves to flow along with the mood of the party. However, they are reluctant to be pushed into corners with everyone's least favourite relative, or made to sit with the crowd from Siberia just because they are good communicators. Water Oxen really are quite intolerant when pushed, and they'll bend all the rules if it's their choice to do so. If you have Water Oxen guests, give them a chance to help you work out the seating plan. Even though you may have sneakily organized this beforehand, let them think they have some say in it. Do invite them to all business functions, don't invite them to family reunions.

WATER TIGER

Water Tigers are acutely sensitive and intuitive, and can be a great support at business lunches with their shrewd, uncanny way of knowing what the outcome will be, and of whom to be suspicious. They tune in to any atmosphere with ease, and will be helpful, obliging and inspiring at the dinner table, preferring to chatter and reflect rather than argue and provoke. They are fiercely independent and hate to be ordered around, so don't make them feel they have to help in the kitchen or force them into eating the last course. Beware of the Water Tiger's need for revenge. If your best friend's partner manages to spill coffee on their clothes, you'll probably find the Water Tiger's paw marks in your bath. Do invite them to difficult business lunches, don't invite them to organized or conventional dinner parties.

WATER RABBIT

You can always spot Rabbit guests because they are usually the ones who do all the gossiping as soon as they have stepped through the front door. Avoiding confrontation, they will rarely actually say anything about themselves, and will change their opinions to match everyone else's. This can be a bit tiresome at dinner parties when the conversation needs challenge and the Rabbits are merely nodding their heads in constant agreement. They are kind and generous and probably the only animals who'll always bring a gift for the host. However, they usually manage to avoid the washing up! Do invite them for informal and impromptu get-togethers, don't invite them to serious conventional dinners.

WATER DRAGON

Water Dragons are totally unmethodical, which makes them terrible hosts, but exciting guests. These are people you can rely on for sparkling conversation, exotic and vitalizing interaction, but don't count on them to be there when you want the candles lit! They are highly confident, but never ready to stay put. They are the most nomadic and transient of all the Dragons, and if the party isn't moving at a changing or volatile pace then they'll quickly become restless and leave. You might not even spot them go. They have a knack of disappearing through a bathroom window, or slipping past the mass of coats in the hall while nimbly grabbing a bottle kindly left on the side table by another arriving guest. Do invite them for lively parties and suppers, don't invite them for slow, serious feasts and dinners.

WATER SNAKE

Dangerous and deadly guests if they are not your closest friends. Make sure you know why you've invited them and check to see if you've ever crossed them in the past, because if you have they'll strike back. These are people who will wait for the right moment to retaliate, so if they are coming to your business do, check out their credentials! However, Water Snakes make excellent guests if you know they are on your side. The right side of their brains are calculating while the left side is intensely intuitive and they are always magnetic, shrewd and intoxicating. With Water Snakes around you don't need much alcohol. They hate big gatherings and prefer places where they can assert their power, which is why they make better hosts than guests. Do invite them to formal dos if you know you can trust them, don't invite them to wild or informal parties.

WATER HORSE

Committing themselves to actually arriving at your party is the first hurdle, the second is whether they'll have enough patience to last it out. Like other Water energy people they really do have a problem with sticking to the rules, but have a natural talent for conversation and charm. Because they live on their nerves, Water Horses may switch sides in business deals and difficult family arguments, simply because they swerve instinctively towards whoever is winning. Great fun at large parties, but may not wait for the soup to be served when faced with a five-course banquet. Do invite them to large parties, don't expect them to turn up!

WATER SHEEP

The guests who walk through the door and complain immediately about the weather, their clothes, the journey or their partner are usually Water Sheep. They are highly sensitive but tend to put a damper on any party if they are feeling particularly moody. Don't invite them to a party of new friends they haven't met before. First, they may freak out about going somewhere with new people, or a different location, and second, even if things are to their taste, they'll still find something to moan about. Ultimately worriers, don't invite them to business lunches and intimate dinner parties, unless you can provide them with a constant supply of laughter, fun or someone who's got worse problems than they have! Do invite them to family get-togethers, weddings and celebrations they're great with difficult relatives.

WATER MONKEY

These guests are either punctual to the second, or so early that they hang around in the car or the pub down the road until the right moment. They are hyperactive and live on their nerves. They may wear two watches and will never look you straight in the eye. It's not that they can't be trusted, just that they can't trust themselves as to what they are thinking or feeling. They really love listening and talk less than other Monkeys, but they can be fickle, so take care if you're planning to let them in on a secret. Do invite them to easy, light occasions, don't invite them to formal or slow and lengthy banquets.

WATER ROOSTER

The gentlest and most artistic of the Rooster family, these guests will admire your works of art, offer inspired ideas for your interior, and then decide you really ought to hang that crystal in the other window. They mean well but often seem arrogant and vain, and usually confuse strangers rather than make them feel at ease. Being alert to the energy and atmosphere of your party, however, they will be useful as influential guests or business associates. Their approach to life is about precision and perfection, so don't overcook the roast or leave your underwear in the bathroom. Do invite them to business lunches and PR parties, don't invite them to impromptu suppers.

WATER DOG

Alluring and fascinating, these are guests that get your party talked about. Without doubt the most free-ranging and non-committal of Dog types. These people want the high life and will play any kind of sophisticated party game just to turn on everyone else with their irresistible sexual aura. Watch out they don't bring unwanted hangers-on, or beautiful friends who appeal to Dog-like appetites. The gentle quality of these guests, however, outweighs their faults and they can be relied upon to amuse and entertain your other guests if the party starts flagging. Water Dogs don't like to go to a party that's anything short of social excellence. Do invite them to glamorous parties or those for 'special' people, don't invite them to informal occasions and bring-a-bottle parties.

WATER PIG

These guests will always want to see the best in everyone they meet and expect every party to be perfect. They are eternal optimists and are great to have around with their stunning ability to communicate with anyone under the sun and their craving for the good life, good food, and good company. You'll recognize them by their habit of holding two plates in one hand, glass in the other, and their faces all smiles at whoever it is who may be taking advantage of their genuinely benevolent nature. They may live with their heads permanently in the clouds, so watch out for spills on the carpet and don't expect them to wipe it up. Do invite them to buffets and cocktail parties, don't invite them to banquets and sit-down formal feasts.

Wood Energy Is Altruistic

WOOD RAT

These people are naturally charming and sociable. They reach out for anything that looks tempting and may well be the first to grab the best piece of salmon off the buffet table, or open the champagne that Uncle George brought for a final toast when the hangers-on have gone. Being clever and quick-witted, they don't have time for charades or long speeches; they'd rather enjoy a game of liar dice, brag, or just play mental games with every other guest to see who can outwit the other. There is usually an ulterior motive for Rats to have parties, and usually a more subtle or sly motive for them to go to one. Do invite them to light-hearted big events, don't invite them to dull business lunches.

WOOD OX

You can usually spot Wood Ox guests from the kitchen, without even knowing your guests' signs, simply because they like to make themselves heard. They live big and often speak big. And often they'll be the ones who can manage to dance all night and still enjoy a glass of champagne at dawn. The network of friends they have means they might be surrounded by their own crowd of hangers-on. Alternatively, they'll know everyone at your party better than you do, and the business lunch you had in mind will turn out to their advantage rather than yours. They don't mean to upset anyone, but somehow they always do. Do invite them to glamorous and noisy parties, don't invite them to intimate tête-à-têtes with a few friends you want to impress yourself.

WOOD TIGER

Formal dinner parties are usually avoided, simply because these Tigers hate dressing up for the sake of convention. Attending a business lunch may fire their enthusiasm to put on a show, but make sure if you invite a Wood Tiger to dinner that they are on your side. They are remarkably gifted at turning conversations into arguments as they can be awkward just for the sake of being awkward. They are also quite capable of pointing out the defects in your culinary skills. They will have many of their own culinary ideas of course, so be prepared for them to bring their own organic vinegar, sauces and bread. They are notoriously set in their eating habits. Don't try to change them, or you may have to rearrange more than the furniture. Do invite them to simple meals where you aren't trying to impress with your cooking, don't invite them to formal dinner parties.

WOOD RABBIT

These Rabbits love their surroundings to be aesthetic and harmonious, so you may find them rearranging your table, your furniture and even suggesting what music to play. They want the world to be an elegant and serene place, and often find parties don't always live up to their high expectations. Frankly, they are difficult to please. As hosts they are more successful, probably because they can organize and embellish the right qualities that make them feel safe in their environment. Harmonious entertaining comes naturally to Rabbits, but Wood

Rabbit guests need to find a balance between their need to escape the real world and their need to actually live in it. Do invite them to cocktail parties and impromptu suppers, don't invite them to contrived parties, or formal banquets and dinners.

WOOD DRAGON

These guests are unlikely to be your favourites unless you enjoy doing battle for hours over the dinner table with their incredible powers of argument. They are always right, and there is little chance for compromise when they're around. You can usually spot them because they walk around looking confident and generally outrageously dressed. They can be highly eccentric and enjoy anything from the smallest soiree to the grandest feast. The world revolves around Wood Dragons, but if you can bear their company they'll bring with them inspirational ideas, aloof glamour, and a charismatic quality to enliven the dullest occasion. They are rich in vision, but can be awfully poor when it comes to thanking you on leaving. After all, didn't they suggest the whole idea for the party to you in the first place? Do invite them to business lunches if you want an air of dissidence, don't invite them to anything highly conventional, or to cocktail parties.

WOOD SNAKE

If you need a public speaker Wood Snakes usually enjoy standing up in front of an audience. They are undoubtedly stimulating and fascinating to have around, but like other Snakes it's best to find out where their loyalties are, and that they are on your side. They are gregarious but highly vain, and somehow have a talent for drawing all the guests to their mysterious and magnetic side. Candlelight and darkness suits them, but watch out, they may decide to set up camp and be the party guru. Do invite them to dinner parties if you want good conversation, don't invite them to large barbecues and buffets.

WOOD HORSE

Wood Horse guests can be the best kind of guests to have, as long as you let them have their space. They respond to most social occasions with ease, and aren't too bothered about what they wear or the kind of impression they give, although this might be awkward for more formal or business occasions. Yet they always appear glamorous even in the most inappropriate and way-out of clothes. Do invite them round for outdoor parties, and late-night informal conversation, don't invite them to dinner parties with intimate friends as they prefer to shock and seduce rather than conform with black ties or party frocks!

WOOD SHEEP

Wood Sheep are the least insecure of all the Sheep family and so you can usually rely on them to be more civilized, outgoing and well dressed. They have oodles of empathy for their fellow guests and may patronize those distant relations in the corner who you really haven't got time for anyway. Preferring large buffets and outdoor-type parties, Wood Sheep aren't particularly interested in the food or the drink, what they are really interested in is how people tick. However, Wood Sheep may get righteous and self-opinionated at intimate dinner parties where their natural talent for grazing around the table is unsustainable.

WOOD MONKEY

These people love prying into everyone else's affairs, and they do so with amazingly direct and often invasive tactics. They are guests with a mission, and they're dazzling, enticing and able to wriggle in and out of the most daunting of situations with ease. If you want conversation, these people are the most brilliant of communicators. However, they assume they know everything, and are extremely passionate orators who may rarely give you a chance to get a word in. Suggest large informal crowds and a bowl of nuts for these guests to take round. Don't give them the bottle to pour or they'll probably stand all night and fill up their own glass while illuminating your friends with their words of wisdom. Do invite them to parties that rely heavily on conversation, don't invite them to dance parties.

WOOD ROOSTER

Unbelievably nit-picking, they are willing to polish all the cutlery with their napkin if they arrive first (which they invariably do, like most Roosters). However, these guests are more flexible than the other Roosters. They enjoy big gatherings where they can flex their communication skills and be in control. For this reason they often make better hosts than guests, so make sure you're ready for the criticism and their ideas on improving your garden as they make a grand entrance through the door. Alternatively, sit them with any Metal guests in your company and watch the fireworks. Do invite them to large informal occasions, don't invite them to spend an evening supper party with home videos.

WOOD DOG

These guests may be better described as Top Dogs, rather than Wood Dogs. They are usually happiest at big social events and lively stimulating parties, or business occasions where the emphasis is on marketing themselves or something they believe in. They have strong convictions and are usually the leaders of the pack, rather than the runts of the litter. If your party is sophisticated and fashionable so much the better, for Wood Dogs thrive on progress and social climbing. They'll avoid the kitchen and won't help with drinks, but they'll probably be there till morning listening to every opinion with tireless loyalty to your cause. Do invite them, as an investment, to your business lunches, don't invite them to dinner parties that aren't on the social ladder.

WOOD PIG

Let these guests organize the invitations, the menu and the entertainment and they'll be your friends for life. These people must help out rather than be helped, and they'll probably prefer taking a firm position of authority in the kitchen or at the front door to actually being a guest. Great as hosts, they find it difficult to take a back seat and be a guest, but if you take advantage of their entrepreneurial skills and their love of creating both the cuisine and the atmosphere, you may never need to worry about the over-cooked pizzas again! Do invite them to small functions, drinks parties and buffets, don't invite them to formal dinner parties.

THE ELEMENTAL ENERGIES AND YOU

As you are the one giving the dinner party or throwing the yearly bash, then it's also essential to take an objective view of yourself as host. Reinforcing your own element is vital for any occasion, so knowing a bit more about the energy you express and the energy to which you resonate can help you become more aware of your own inbuilt fallibility circuit as well as those you may have already discovered of your guests.

FIRE HOST

If you're Fire you'll probably get your party organized in a flash, and you'll be impulsive about your choice of food, guests and timing. The way you tune in to your guests depends on their sense of fun and adventure. If they're stuffy and dull you'll work hard to liven them up, but you may tire of them quickly. If they're wise and witty you'll find their company stimulating, but you may have to resist trying to take over the conversation.

Food and drink will have to be fast to eat, with little to clear up after. Intimate dinner parties will be fine if you're the centre of attention, but if you're not, you may disappear into the garden. Wild and big gatherings mean you can move freely from person to person and keep up the momentum, pleasing the dynamic and often impatient side of your nature. Your biggest test will be in keeping yourself from making tactless remarks, being too pushy with the drinks and the nibbles or getting bored by aged relatives. The kind of host who circulates well, you'll be lively and open to turning your party into an adventure, but don't insist that everyone has to be as exuberant as you.

EARTH HOST

You probably have a head start on the other elements in that you like to nurture others and to receive them into your home without much fuss. Panic rarely sets in when faced with an important lunch to impress guests and you're usually organized and prepared days ahead of schedule. You'll love being the earthy pleasure-giving host. The one who has thought of simply everything! From the champagne on ice (if you can afford it) to the tea ceremony (if you can't). You'll take your time to welcome your guests one by one and never let on if you get exhausted by their company. Being highly capable in the kitchen you may find you don't need anyone else's help on the great day. Your biggest test is to keep the mood swinging, and to go with the flow when it seems to move in the right direction. Resistance to others may mean you appear aloof and righteous, the kind of host who keeps the best bottle of Chardonnay in the back of the fridge for the right guests! Earth hosts usually give the impression they've taken no trouble at all to arrange the most extraordinary feast of delights. You are remarkably independent and like to indulge yourself in observing everyone else's pleasure. A seasoned party giver, you prefer to watch your guests enjoy themselves rather than join in, unless you have a chance to tell the same old jokes over and over again.

METAL HOST

Not known for your gregarious nature, when you need to entertain you will do so in the best possible and most lavish style. Your need to entertain will usually be when you have some ambition to fulfil, whether it's a promotion, a social climb with those in the know or merely the desire to indulge your fantasies in the most outrageous party your friends have ever attended. There is power to be had as a host, and this can lead you into entertaining for many different kinds of objectives. However, once you have decided to become involved with any event you can become quite compulsive and intensely passionate about the whole occasion. You need the company of those you can trust. Strangers may prove to be too suspect, but close relatives are not necessarily of importance to you. However, family reunions may come up more often than you like and this is where your extraordinary powers of regeneration and dedication mean you'll make even the dullest party an extraordinary success. You're the kind of host who may not be particularly popular, but is always fascinating.

WATER HOST

Being so sensitive to your guests' emotions, you may find you end up flapping around all night from kitchen to loo, from garden to telephone, in an attempt to fulfil everyone else's needs rather than your own. A whizz at creating an imaginative and harmonious setting, you may find, however, that you're out of balance with yourself. However gregarious and charming you are, your guests will usually adore you, until of course you start flirting with those dull business colleagues who never seem to have a sense of humour. This may get you into trouble, but it may also get you a reputation for being an unpredictable, scatty, yet wonderfully sociable party thrower. Whether you really want to be as beguiling and fluid as others make you out is questionable. Your biggest challenge may be the grandest and biggest dos, simply because with all those people to entertain how are you ever going to have time to be charming to them all?

WOOD HOST

Without doubt the Wood Host can turn even the most informal and impromptu occasion into a glamorous or sophisticated event. You may have eccentric ideas about the food, the presentation and even the time of day – some Wood hosts prefer early morning breakfasts and brunches to evening parties – but somehow people are drawn to your stylish and unconventional approach to entertaining in an easy manner. Being more concerned with the aesthetics of the event rather than the actual pleasure of it, may mean your poise can be a little off-balance when confronted with business lunches which don't seem to be going anywhere except further down the wine list. You'll prefer social informality, tending towards an open-house approach, because once you start to lay the table the chances are you'll be far more interested in the possibilities of experimenting with the table-leg height. Wood hosts are best at organizing big parties where they have a number of invaluable helpers. Wood organization is never slapdash, it is ambitious.

WHO IS YIN OR YANG?

Yin and Yang determine how each of your guests may express their energy, either directly (Yang) or indirectly (Yin). If you find that most of your guests are Yang people, for example, and you are the only Yin person then you may need to reinforce your energy. This is not because Yang is more powerful than Yin. They both have equal power, but the energy is expressed in different ways. What needs balancing is the fusion of the two energies so that the atmosphere is harmonious and not one-sided.

SO WHO GETS ON WITH WHO?

If you look at the Cycle of Elements diagram on page 7 you'll see there is a creative cycle and a destructive cycle. Below is a chart based on these cycles to show you how the different elements cope with each other.

IF YOU ARE:	HARMONIOUS	NOT SO HARMONIOUS
FIRE	Fire Wood Earth	Water Metal
EARTH	Metal Fire Earth	Water Wood
METAL	Water Earth Metal	Wood Fire
WATER	Water Metal Wood	Fire Earth
WOOD	Wood Fire Water	Metal Earth

Chart of Harmonious and not so harmonious contacts

HOW TO BALANCE THE DIFFERENT ENERGIES OF YOUR GUESTS

The simplest way to ensure harmony at the dinner table or party is always to make up the balance of deficient energies with specific cures and remedies for those elements. For example, in a dinner party of six, if you have three Fire guests, two Water guests, and you are Earth:

Fire is strongest here and there is no Metal or Wood. In this case you could enhance the centre of the table with the strength of Metal candlesticks, without the candles (too much Fire), but using pieces of gnarled wood in the candlesticks instead. As a table decoration this also provides the necessary two missing elements without being too powerful or overwhelming on the table. Obviously, there may be a wooden table and chairs, so Wood energy is often the last element you need to worry about in your interior, unless of course you prefer metal or plastic furniture.

IF THERE IS LITTLE OR NO FIRE Dress the table with plenty of candles, a red tablecloth and warm enriching colour schemes. Create a dynamic atmosphere with lighting, unusual food, or exotic tableware.

IF THERE IS LITTLE OR NO WATER Use soft blue candles, and add greys and blacks in your decoration. Keep the lighting simple, diffused and gentle. Give guests fingerbowls and sprinkle silver glitter in the water to sparkle in the candlelight.

IF THERE IS LITTLE EARTH Add yellows, ochres and coffee colours to your decoration. Use rich brown glass candleholders and chunky church candles if you want candlelight. Incorporate flowers, gourds, seed pods and unusual arrangements of fruit or whole spices.

Who Sits Next To Who?

This can be tricky if you have, say, Fire and Water guests and no other element represented to balance these. However, although they are not notoriously the best of friends, in a way putting these two guests together can provide challenging and stimulating conversation. On the other hand, although having seemingly similar ways of expressing themselves, two Earth guests together could provide a rather dull corner of the table, as they both tend to get on with the pleasures of eating rather than sparkling conversation.

Use the compatibility chart on page 61 to work out the best combinations for small parties. Obviously, the more the merrier, and the more balanced guest-wise the party becomes.

Auspicious Directions

Every element has a best direction in which to face, and from which they also receive beneficial energy. Obviously if you've got four Fire guests they aren't all going to be able to sit facing south at the same time unless you've got an awfully big table and like awkward seating arrangements.

It's best to work with yourself first. As the host, you're the one who must feel the most auspicious energy coming your way. Once you have ensured that you are in harmony, your guests will be suitably balanced. However, if you know you have a difficult relation, business colleague or awkward stranger to entertain, then try to ensure they are sitting in an auspicious direction that aligns with your Bagua. Difficult people need handling with care, whereas easygoing friends may not need that extra energy boost just for one evening. So don't worry about seating them all in the right directions! Business lunches and important dinners, whether romantic or social, will benefit from placing key guests in the right direction.

FIRE people are best placed facing south or east

EARTH·people are best placed facing south-west or north-east.

METAL people are best placed facing west or north-west

WATER people are best place facing north or south

WOOD people are best placed facing east or south-east.

Auspicious Directions for Difficult Guests

The Bagua

FIRE people are best placed in the seat which corresponds to Disclosure.

EARTH people are best placed in the seat which corresponds to Tolerance or Being Cool.

METAL people are best place in the seat which corresponds to Friendship or Pleasure.

WATER people are best placed in the seat which corresponds to Flow or Disclosure.

WOOD people are best placed in the seat which corresponds to Initiative or Prosperity.

Uninvited Guests

Sometimes your best friend, colleague, or partner may turn up with an uninvited guest at the last minute. This is someone you can do nothing about. You can't exactly confront them on the doorstep with a piece of amber for them to hold all evening to soak up any negative energy they may be carrying. Neither are you likely to ask them outright their date of birth, unless, of course, you are a Fire Horse, Water Monkey or Metal Dragon!

The easiest option for dealing with these guests is to use a remedy from the selection below, depending on what is available at short notice, and the kind of entertaining you have in mind.

If you can find out their birth date and elemental energy, then use the enhancements according to their element.

Unknown Element or Energy

Use:

1. The well-known European cure for warding off vampires can be used with equal success with uninvited guests. They may be perfectly charming and genuine people, but they are bringing a new and potentially disturbing energy into your home. So hang a string of garlic near your kitchen door, or place a few cloves of garlic in a small stone bowl and position subtly near the entrance or where they hang their coats.

2. If you have a piece of amber, even if it's a necklace, or ear-ring, place this in the window or on a ledge opposite to where the uninvited guest is sitting. Amber has a remarkable ability to draw in difficult energy and its vibrational healing energy will complement even the most dubious of strangers.

3. Make sure you have a mirror opposite your own seat at the table: this will reflect the back of your uninvited guest's head and hopefully ensure their aura is contained by your own visual ch'i. Remember, ch'i is the energy that flows through everything and everyone, and like meridians in acupuncture, this ch'i travels through sight, conversation and all the other senses.

If You Know Their Element

Cures, remedies and energizers for difficult guests:

FIRE – Place a wooden bird in your entertaining room.

EARTH – Place an octagonal mirror on your window ledge.

METAL – Place a paperweight beside your entrance door.

WATER – Place a pewter, brass or bronze item on your side table.

WOOD – Place a bowl of water filled with floating candles in your entertaining room.

Number Energy

There are two ways of determining a guest's numerological and energy resonance. In Feng Shui there are also numbers which correspond to your year of birth relating to the Bagua. However, this means you would have to ask your guest for their birth date anyway, so here is a Western system for finding a number to which people resonate and one which seems to work mysteriously well. I am therefore combining Eastern and Western energy resonances. Below is an alphabetical code. Each letter corresponds to a number. Simply add up the numbers of your guest's name as in the example and keep adding until you end up with a number between 1 and 9. This will give you a key number of the Bagua that will be just as important for their energy flow as their birth element, or animal sign.

Use this number to determine which area of the Bagua to sit them in, or look up in the Bagua chart below which element this Bagua number resonates to so that you can work with their element as well as the Bagua.

Example of use: Let's say your mystery guest is called Jackie Smith (always use the name they prefer to be called by).

1	2	3	4	5	6	7	8	9
A	B	C	D	E	F	G	H	I
J	K	L	M	N	O	P	Q	R
S	T	U	V	W	X	Y	Z	

$1+1+3+2+9+5+1+4+9+2+8 = 45$ then $4+5 = 9$

So 9 is Jackie Smith's Bagua number.

Chart of Bagua with elements associated

1	Flow	North	Water
2	Tolerance	South-west	Earth
3	Initiative	East	Wood
4	Prosperity	South-east	Wood
5	Connections	All Directions	Any Element
6	Friendship	North-west	Metal
7	Pleasure	West	Metal
8	Being Cool	North-east	Earth
9	Disclosure	South	Fire

You now know that Jackie Smith's number is 9. Her Bagua location is Disclosure, and Fire is her 'number element'. It would probably be most appropriate to seat her in the area of the table that corresponds to Disclosure. Her number element is Fire.

Always remember the golden rule, don't let any one element dominate.

Compatibility chart

Use this chart to give you a quick and easy glance at the guests' compatibility rating. Those marked with a Dragon Star are particularly excellent combinations and those with a Black Moon less easy combinations.

BLACK MOON ● Uneasy

DRAGON STAR ★ Easy

	WOMAN FIRE	WOMAN EARTH	WOMAN METAL	WOMAN WATER	WOMAN WOOD
MAN FIRE	★★ ★	★ ★	● ●	● ● ●	★
MAN EARTH	★ ★	★	★ ★ ★	● ●	● ● ●
MAN METAL	● ● ●	★ ★ ★	★	★ ★	● ●
MAN WATER	● ● ●	● ● ●	★ ★	★	★ ★ ★
MAN WOOD	★ ★	● ●	● ● ●	★ ★ ★	★

CHAPTER THREE

Formal Dinners

SETTING THE MOOD

Unlike celebrations, house-warmings and informal parties, formal dinner parties often disguise all kinds of exciting, inspiring, and unusual motives for having one. This is why the purpose and the mood you want to create must be always kept in mind.

In Chapter Six you will discover five different moods to create for dinner parties if you need specific inspiration. However, even if you know exactly the kind of atmosphere you are aiming for, energize yourself first before you even handle the accessories.

ENERGIZE YOURSELF

Like any stage play, your dinner party is about performance, art and script. It's also about lighting, scenery and props. But first ensure that you as director are Feng Shui wise.

Find out your birth element on page 9 and look up the kind of host you are. Follow the guide below depending on your element to ensure you are prepared and energized accordingly.

FIRE — choose a painting, image or photo that is predominantly red and place it in the bathroom or toilet that guests are most likely to use. Wear something red, even if you aren't fond of the colour (it could be underwear, it doesn't have to be obvious to your guests).

EARTH — in your hallway place a large jug of dried wooden branches, or swirls of sculptural leaves or dried seed pods. Wear an earthy fragrance, and dab it around the house as well as on your body.

METAL — either use a tiny wooden or terracotta bowl and fill with gold beads, silver coins or metal rings, anything which suggests your own element. Place in your bedroom. Also ensure you wear gold or silver next to your skin, but somewhere that is secret.

WATER — place a glass bowl of water in the bathroom or toilet and cover the surface with flower heads — either blue or white petals, whichever are in season. Also ensure you wear a piece of amber next to your skin, as jewellery or placed in a pocket.

WOOD — with a silver-coloured pen, write down a favourite poem or quotation on a piece of ochre or green-coloured hand-made paper. Attach it to the wall of your hallway so that guests will be unable to resist reading it. Use patchouli incense while you bathe.

FENG SHUI TIP

If you are hosting a formal dinner party with your partner, remember that his or her energy is as important as your own. Find out their elemental energy as well and place an energizer from the list below in a secret place near to where you are cooking or serving. This will ensure that you are both balanced, whether your partner is a Feng Shui advocate or not.

IF YOUR PARTNER IS FIRE: a red scarf, small mirror, a bell, or red glass.

IF YOUR PARTNER IS EARTH: a piece of yellow citrine, a fossil or beautiful stone from the garden, a honeycomb or bundle of whole spices.

IF YOUR PARTNER IS METAL: a metal candlestick, a black and white photo of friends, brass rubbing, gold thread, or silver coins.

IF YOUR PARTNER IS WATER: a fountain pen, a piece of amber or turquoise, a blue candle, a cup of blue-coloured water.

IF YOUR PARTNER IS WOOD: a wooden bird, a paper dragon, a pot of herbs, or a piece of malachite.

What To Wear?

What you wear sometimes seems to take on major proportions. Depending on the guests and the purpose of the occasion you may tear your hair out as you try on fifty different numbers, then settle again for that little black dress, or you may rush out and impulse buy on something sexy or fashionable. Whatever the method you arrive at for your choice of clothes, try to wear on your person one of the following stones or crystals for maximum self-confidence, success and charisma. If you don't have these stones or crystals, then choose a colour from the ones suggested to wear somewhere on your body.

FIRE – carnelian or bloodstone. Best colour: red

EARTH – smoky quartz or moonstone. Best colour: autumnal hues

METAL – diamond or obsidian. Best colour: silver, gold or black

WATER — lapis lazuli or amber. Best colour: deep blues, blacks and purples

WOOD — malachite or green tourmaline. Best colour: green

THE INVITATION

Depending on the mood you are trying to create it is essential to send out the energy from the start via your invitations, so that even before your guests arrive they are already aware of the ambience you wish to create. Invitations are often prized possessions on the wall or notice board, mantelpiece or shelf. Make sure your invites are equal to the occasion.

If you are going to impress:
Use simple bold designs, black on white and no frilly edges. But always make sure you have some curving lines on the invite, either the writing or some design you have incorporated into the border — perhaps just one motif in one corner. This is because beneficial energy flows in spirals and curves and difficult energy, called 'secret arrow' energy, usually travels in straight lines. If you are inviting work colleagues and employers for the first time into your home (see Chapter Eight for business and corporate entertaining) then maximize your chances of success by indulging in formal invitations scribed with gold.

If you are going to delight:
For important guests suggest a hint of what is to come by impressing the invitation with a fragrance that could be suggestive of the mood of the dinner party.

Here are a few ideas for fragrances you can use for different moods. Use essential oils, or perfume and dab some on to the invite with your finger just before you pop it in the envelope.

For delightful fun use sandalwood
For delightful communication use lemon verbena
For delightful flirtation use white musk
For delightful bores use patchouli
For delightful VIPS use hyacinth

If you are going to show off

Many of us have dinner parties just to flaunt our culinary skills, our husbands, wives or home. Even if we've just finished the decorating and the builders have finally gone, it's a chance to revel in our own taste and hope our friends will drool. For these invitations use your imagination and bring an element of your particular 'show-off' into the invite to subtly flaunt it before they get there.

For example, if you're longing to christen the new wine glasses you received as a wedding present, send an invite shaped like your glasses, or draw or use photo images of wine glasses on the blank card before you write. By sending out the energy in advance, even in this simple visual form, your guests will arrive with expectations of the joy of being in your company.

PRE-DINNER ENHANCEMENTS

Formal dinners require a great deal more effort than just a quick visit to the supermarket. They often involve a complete culinary schedule as well as shopping, cleaning, and the panic of polishing and decorating two or three days or so ahead of time. This may be where you feel most under pressure, so use some Feng Shui tips to ensure you and your home are energized accordingly.

SHOPPING – Put a small silk pouch or scarf in your pocket or bag filled with rosemary or lavender to keep you calm and sane.

COOKING — Place some cloves of garlic, or hang a string of garlic above your microwave to disperse the difficult energy that microwaves emit. You'll probably be using your microwave a lot, so always make sure you have garlic near this highly potent source of energy to counterbalance its effects. Garlic is a purifier, so use it liberally. If using a conventional oven, hang a bunch of keys or a keyring on the wall to the left of the cooker to empower you with self-confidence.

UNCLUTTER AND CLEAN — Get your mop out and get on with it.

THE NIGHT-BEFORE RITUAL — Bathe in musky bath oils and place a piece of amber on the window ledge of your entertaining room to draw away all the difficult or disturbing energies from the day. When you go to bed place a small bowl of stones near your bed to ground you ready for the extra energy you need for the next day.

THE TABLE

The table is the most important part of your dinner-party energy. It both grounds those who sit before it, and supports the food about to be eaten. Tables are like rocks and stones, they must be solid and willing to support, yet strong enough to draw in our many confusing emotional and spiritual energies.

Shapes and Sharing

The whole ritual of sharing food has played an important part in every culture for thousands of years. The Chinese have their own customs regarding table manners and courtesy, and their own preferences for how they eat, and what they eat. The suggestions in this book are based on the principles of ancient Chinese philosophy, but draw on our own traditions and modern methods of entertaining. Therefore, these Feng Shui harmonizers and balancers suit our contemporary lifestyle, and the ideas, images and use of style outlined in this book are very much aligned to this. Do you really want your house to turn into a Chinese palace?

What is important is to combine a balance of Yin and Yang in your environment for the happiness of all who eat and share food at your table. Below are some diagrams of auspicious tables and furniture arrangements, and also some inauspicious ones.

Although round tables are better for energy flow, square and oblong tables are more common in our society, so my suggestions are ways of bringing the dynamic of both Yin (soft, flowing energy) and Yang (straight, direct energy) into balance. You do not have to have a round table for success!

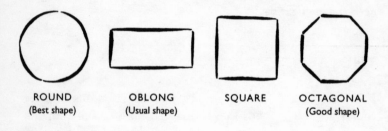

ROUND
(Best shape)

OBLONG
(Usual shape)

SQUARE

OCTAGONAL
(Good shape)

Most tables are made of wood. So you are off to a good start with Wood energy, which enables others to participate freely, without feeling restricted or judged. Some people prefer metal and glass tables, and these are fine, as long as you bring in some Wood element into the room to counteract the cold and somewhat harsh energy of Metal. However, metal tables and chairs can be of great benefit if you are trying to impress your employer, friends or relatives. The strength of Metal will support the sense of your integrity and what you are trying to achieve.

To balance too much Metal furniture

Hang a still-life painting, abstract or realistic, on a wall in your entertaining room. Alternatively place a bowl of delectable exotic fruits beside your entertaining-room door.

If you have an odd number of guests

The simple solution for balancing a table with an odd number of chairs (unless of course you have a round table) is to place an empty chair to complete the balance of numbers on either side. An empty chair diffuses the negative energy that an imbalance of numbers may create. The only exception to this is the Crystal Dinner Party suggested in Chapter Six of this book (page 144) when the number five is especially important.

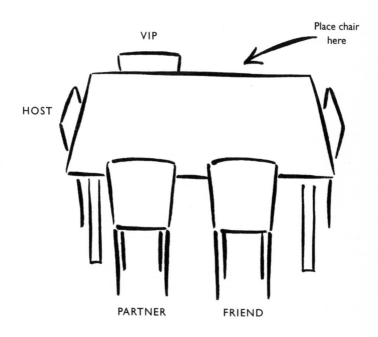

THE ROOM

Auspicious room

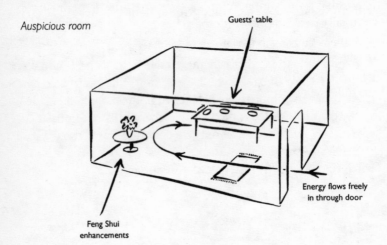

Guests' table

Feng Shui
enhancements

Energy flows freely
in through door

Inauspicious room

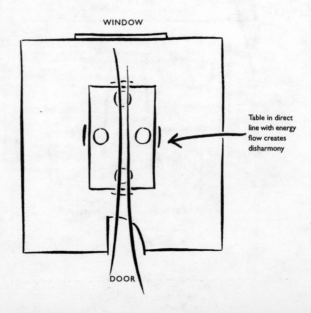

WINDOW

Table in direct
line with energy
flow creates
disharmony

DOOR

As you are the host avoid sitting with your back to the door. This is one of the most negative positions for anyone to sit in. If possible make sure no one has their back to the door. Short of totally rearranging your furniture, hang a small image, picture or photo of a storm, sunset, lightning or wild weather on the wall opposite the vulnerable position, as in the diagram below. This will create a powerful energy-circuit breaker for the vulnerable guest!

Worst place for sitting at table

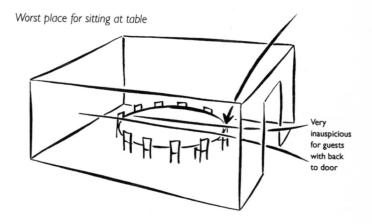

Very inauspicious for guests with back to door

Best place for sitting at table

These four guests all have a view of the door

DOORWAY

Sometimes there is little you can do to change the layout of the furniture in the room, but the following suggestions may bring you success at these rather formal functions.

1. Try to ensure that you as the host have behind you a powerful colour, a flat wall, perhaps a display of coloured glasses, a gigantic painting or a wall hanging. This provides stability and prevents you receiving difficult energy from behind. This area is known as your Tortoise energy, as it is essential to protect your back from attack and you need a strong shell, like a coat of armour, to defend you.

2. To your left, place an upright object, such as a tall plant, wooden sculpture or an image of rising smoke, spirals or even a dragon or dragonfly images, anything that suggests opening out to the world, liberation and generosity. This is known as the area of the Dragon and corresponds to liberal acceptance.

3. To your right, place a small table or a low stool. If you have another guest seated to your right, then you could just put a small rug on the floor or even lay an extra napkin on the table. Your right side is about how you control the environment and also the boundaries you create both emotionally and physically. This is where your Tiger energy waits.

4. The area directly in front of you is known as the Phoenix. This is the energy of possibilities, of foresight and your enthusiasm for the future, it is your pathway towards success and enjoyment.

COLOURS

Fashion may dictate which colours are best for decorating your table. However, there are certain colours which give out and ingest certain energies. Depending on how formal the occasion is and who your chosen guests are you must decide which of the colours are dominant, and which are merely back-up colours to keep the energy balanced. Remember, don't let any one energy dominate!

CHECKS AND PATTERNS – great for joviality and a less formal approach if you want to take the sting out of difficult occasions.

REDS/ORANGES/YELLOWS – these are Fire and Earth energies, perfect for inspiring passionate conversation, and adding verve to your cuisine. Reds stimulate everyone's appetites, so be sure to have plenty of food in that oven when dressing your table in red!

BLUES – this is cooling and subduing energy. For sophisticated dinners this is a superb colour for a tablecloth, but use with caution. Blue tends to suppress the appetite, and often induces the desire to drink instead! Keep the champagne flowing for blue.

GREENS – tranquillity and communication. There could be serious talk when this range of colours is introduced, but the evening will be cool, unconventional and free from malice. Greens don't stimulate heavy eating, so a good colour for fine cuisine and culinary skills to be enjoyed. Quality here without too much quantity.

BLACK – mysterious energy to add to any dinner table. As a table-cloth it could add wicked undercurrents if topped with white candles, white plates and napkins. If you want to cause a sensation, try it! Use black carefully with strangers, and cautiously if you are trying to impress. Black is highly potent, but also highly unstable.

GOLD, WHITE – this is vibrant energy and excellent for high-powered formality. On its own, white is cooling and sophisticated, and gold is highly rewarding and enriching, but together they make for indulgence and excess. The wine is sure to run out!

LIGHTING

If you have a central light above the table, either a chandelier or low pendant hanging lamp, then this is ideal for formal dinners. However, ensure that the light does not obscure your view of the guests, or the guests of you. Soft lighting and low-wattage bulbs are essential.

Bright light will make formal occasions stiff, rigid and the energy stagnate. You may find your guests eat every morsel on their plates, but they won't find it easy to relax with the energy.

Candles provide the most evocative and natural light – and although these are obviously ideal for intimate occasions, creating mood and atmosphere, they may also be used for formal dinners with the right use of colour and number.

Instead of the usual one or two candlesticks on the dinner table, try at least six candles, if you have the space. If not, group ten or more candles on a side table or sideboard, preferably on your Tiger side (to your right) and have mostly whites and cream colours. Yellow is fine, but avoid reds, oranges, blues and purples as these create too intense an energy for formal parties.

THE INTERIOR

Again, work primarily with balancing the elements to keep the energy flowing.

You may, for example, choose white candles, a blue tablecloth and yellow flowers in jugs around the room. Here both lighting and colour, form and nature bring the five elements into the environment with subtlety, rather than using any obvious Feng

Shui decorations such as dragons, talismans or wind chimes.

So, in this example white candles – Metal and Fire together; blue tablecloth – Water; yellow flowers – Wood; terracotta jugs – Earth.

Balancing Act

Formality has to be balanced with informality, so try to bring an element of spontaneity into any overly conventional environment. It can be extremely subtle, but it will be an asset.

Place the following surprise elements in the area of the room which corresponds to the Bagua energy Friendship (see Chapter One on how to place the Bagua).

Depending on the house's own energy these are the choice of surprise elements to enliven your Friendship area. Look at the diagram on page 86 in Chapter One to remind you how to work out your home's principle direction. Whichever direction the energy is flowing in to your house is the principal direction of your home.

If the principal direction of your house is:

NORTH – place a red candle in a metal candlestick and make sure you light it well in advance of the guests' arrival. Put it in the south side of your entertaining room.

SOUTH – place a small bowl of water filled with white flower heads floating on the surface. Place this on the north side of the entertaining room.

EAST – place a metal wall sconce, a gilt-framed mirror or picture on an east wall of the entertaining room.

WEST – place a wooden box, beads, or sculpture in the west area of your entertaining room.

THE ENTRANCE

For formal dinners the entrance to your home is where you usually welcome your guests. If you don't have a separate hallway then use the same energizers in the first room that your guests walk into.

Earth energy brings serenity, poise and above all ensures each guest is centred on arrival. Whoever the guest, even if they are a difficult or unknown factor in your dinner arrangements, this energizer will ensure that they feel comfortable and 'au fait' with the occasion – personality clashes aside!

Place one of the following suggestions in a corner position of the hall or welcoming room facing the doorway to add stability and reinforce Earth energy:

- A piece of quartz crystal, preferably rose or smoky quartz
- A jug of seasonal flowers, berries or fruits
- A bonsai tree or miniature landscape
- A glass jar filled with smooth pebbles
- Antique clock, fabric, tapestries or a richly coloured throw.

THE KITCHEN

If you have stainless-steel utensils, before the dinner party ensure your favourite ones (knives, slicers, ladles, whisks, anything you like but are not using for the party) are placed in a large stone or terracotta jar and stand this on a shelf near the oven. Chrome, silver and cast iron will do just as well, but stainless steel has a higher charge of energy then these other metals.

If you prefer your utensils hanging from hooks remember this is only an energizer for your dinner party. So put a few in a pot just for the occasion. This is Metal energy, and will reinforce your own sense of polish, organization and timing in the kitchen while you work through the menu, get food out of the oven on time and generally attempt to be the perfect host.

The other important balancing element in your kitchen for important formal dinners is Water. Make sure you have a frosted cocktail glass dressed with sticks, fruit, cherries and a sumptuous mix of your favourite liqueur, spirits or mixers to sip through a straw before you start working. Alcohol aside, a luxurious drink, whether a stimulant or not, reinforces refining and cleansing, flowing and being. Even a glass of mineral water is fine, but make sure you use the most precious and beautiful glass you can find!

THE LOO

For formal dinner parties your loo will of course be spotless and the lid and seat always shut! Basic Feng Shui principle. However, you know your guests are more than likely going to visit this private place, so install an energizer to stabilize the effects of different energies being flushed out.

Place a bowl of pebbles or stones that you have found in the garden or polished stones bought from a shop on top of the loo (if the surface is flat, if not, on the window sill or higher surface). Don't place at ground level for this diffuses the energy.

THE DINNER TABLE

The Chinese often dine at round tables and obviously this has the advantage of no one appearing to take precedence over anyone else. It also means that the food is equally shared. In many Chinese restaurants there is usually a round revolving serving dish in the centre for each guest to take their own food when they require it without bothering anyone else.

However, your dinner party does not have to be oriental style to succeed. As the chances are you probably have a square or oblong table then take advantage of its natural strength and stability (four corners, like the four points of the compass, and wooden legs means you have both Earth energy and Wood energy in good supply).

A setting for an oblong table with six or eight guests or a square table with four will usually look like one of the diagrams opposite.

FENG SHUI TIP

Incorporate into the middle of this setting a special circle of candles, decorations, flowers or *objets d'art* to bring in the symbolism of the roundness and give a specific core of unity to the centre of the table Bagua.

Diagram of six at table.

*Diagram of four
at square table*

Seating Layouts

Depending on the occasion you will have to jiggle with where you place your guests. Obviously with family and friends it will be a matter of personal knowing who gets on with who (see the section below for harmonizing guests). But for the purpose of unknown guests always work on the premise that you, as host, will sit at the head of the table and seat the most honoured guest in the area that corresponds to the Bagua area of Initiative. (In the East it is usually considered that the left of the host is the most honoured position, particularly in Malaysia and Singapore, although in Hong Kong left and right vary.) So, place your VIP on the left side but *two seats away* from you. This area of the Bagua is highly potent for advancement, honour and respect and your guest will feel the energy enhancement, even if they don't actually know it! If you have more than one VIP guest, then alternate them with others round the table for maximum respect.

Diagram of alternating VIPS

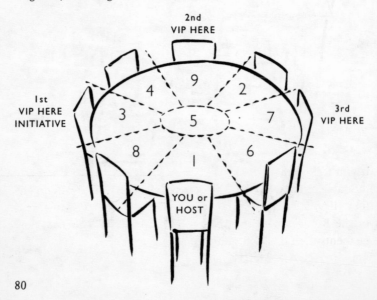

USING THE BAGUA

Draw a rough plan of the shape of your table as shown below, and place the Bagua map over it.

As you are the host, you will generally want to sit near the food supply, but without your back to the door, so first ensure Flow is positioned on the end of the table where you are sitting.

The table

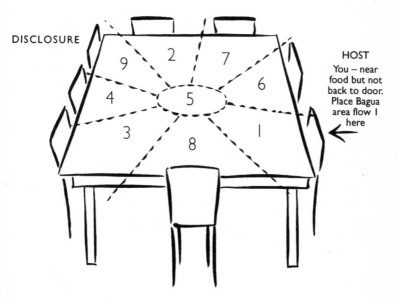

DISCLOSURE

HOST
You – near food but not back to door. Place Bagua area flow 1 here

If you follow the age-old premise of boy, girl, boy, girl around the table, ensure that you've sorted out your VIP arrangement first (if you have any) and then place your guests in the area of the Bagua where they can benefit most. If you know their elements then this will guide you. For example:

FIRE guests are better placed in the seats that correspond to the areas, 3, 4, or 9 (depending on number of seats and people of course).

EARTH guests are better placed in the seats that are in the Bagua areas 2, 8, or 6.

METAL guests are better placed in the seats that correspond to areas 6, 7, or 2.

WATER guests are better placed in the seats that correspond to areas 1, 7 or 8.

WOOD guests are better placed in the seats that correspond to areas 3, 4 or 1.

This is not as complicated as it looks! If you have mostly Fire and Water guests, and you can't fit them all into their appropriate seating positions as they'd all be sitting on top of each other, try as a remedy to balance their positions. You will probably have mostly Wood in the room anyway, so use Earth and Metal to complement their difficult seating positions. If you have Metal furniture, then you would bring in Wood cures.

If there is an imbalance of guest energies, bring into the entertaining room the following energizers depending on which elements are lacking:

IF YOU NEED MORE WATER – use sapphire blue glass

IF YOU NEED MORE FIRE – use a sun-shaped mirror or frame

IF YOU NEED MORE WOOD – use a wooden box or chest

IF YOU NEED MORE METAL – use a dish of chrome or silver balls

IF YOU NEED MORE EARTH – use a grouping of large pebbles.

Some Yin foods for dinner parties

Tomatoes	White fish	Cucumber
Asparagus	Beansprouts	Mint
Mushrooms	Clams	Tofu
Broccoli	Crab	Oysters
Celery	Prawns	

Some Yang foods for dinner parties

Beef	Liver	Smoked fish
Pork	Eggs	Onions
Rabbit	Red peppers	Butter
Turkey	Green peppers	

Finally, ensure you have ONE neutral food in the menu. Choose from the following:

Bread	Green beans	Cauliflower
Rice	Carrots	Garlic
Peas		

TABLEWARE

Choose fine cutlery, linen napkins and simple crockery. If you have the chance to use cut glass, make sure there are two glasses per guest even if you only intend them drinking out of one! This maximizes the energy of Fire, without resorting to more candles if you really haven't got the room.

Cutlery with wooden handles is fine if you need to reinforce Wood in the energy balance. However, there is usually so much Wood in a room anyway that it may be better to opt for knives and forks with silver, metal, or man-made handles.

Paper napkins are OK if you're really stuck, but use them

creatively. Hide a small piece of paper inside the folded napkin with SECRET written on the outside. When they unfold the secret, make sure you have placed a small pressed leaf or flower petals inside, or dabbed a piece of handmade paper with your favourite fragrance. Cool, sophisticated scents are better for formal dinners, and won't disturb the intoxicating smells of your cooking and cuisine.

FINISHING DINNER

Always be sure you are the last to leave the table, and if you are moving into a different room then close the door after you to prevent the stagnant energy of the now chaotic dinner table from going with you. If you have a chance, light an aroma-therapy candle or oil, or burn incense in the room before retiring to bed.

PLACING DIFFICULT GUESTS

If you know that the boss's wife is a quiet mousy type and may prefer to sit silently picking at crumbs all evening, or perhaps she's a bit of a know-it-all and you'd rather she was toned down a little to suit the occasion and not embarrass anyone, then you can place her in a seat which can benefit you both. Here are the choices!

Place the Bagua over the table to ensure that you balance your difficult guest with the correct position:

Noisy guests who need to be toned down – Place them in the seat that corresponds to the Bagua location Tolerance.

Quiet guests who need to be livened up – Place them in the seat that corresponds to the Bagua location Prosperity.

Guests who eat too much – Place them in Friendship!

Guests who don't seem to enjoy eating – Place them in Pleasure.

Guests who are too cynical – Place them in Being Cool.

Guests who don't have any respect – Place them in Initiative.

Guests who constantly nit-pick – Place them in Disclosure.

Guests who don't want to be there – There are occasions when you might need to place guests at the apparent head of the table in your Flow area. This is because they may have only come out of respect for you, or been forced into the occasion through their partner, or it might be that they are highly unpredictable and need to feel they can leave quickly if the mood takes them. In your Flow position they should receive positive energy to stay, and yet still feel free from commitment.

Guests who are gossips – If you really want to hear the inside stories and local gossip, then ensure these guests sit in Disclosure!

CHAPTER FOUR

Romance and the Pleasures of Love

This chapter is devoted to entertaining for love, and how to ensure that you, your partner and the occasion will delight, transform and bring harmony to any romantic or intimate occasion. We have always used food as a romantic energizer. The early ancient Eastern civilizations were highly skilled with herbs, spices and aphrodisiacs to ensure that the balance of opposites – Yin and Yang, male and female – were united in perfect union and happiness.

Depending on which stage of your relationship you are at there are different sections to tempt you. You may be eager to seduce, to attract, to propose or to just have fun. You may be deeply involved in a love affair, whether clandestine or not. On the other hand you may want to call the whole thing off and don't know how to do it with grace. Whatever your intimate reason for sharing food, drink and pleasure, use this guide to get the most out of who you are, your relationship and to bring both harmony and fulfilment to you and your partner.

ENERGIZE YOURSELF AND THE ENVIRONMENT FOR ROMANCE

These energizers and enhancements are all appropriate for entertaining in your home. If you choose to go out to a neutral environment, i.e. a restaurant, bistro or bar, to begin a romantic liaison then look in the later section in this chapter.

You may have met in the office, the train or on the dance floor, but whatever your first encounter, inviting him/her to your home is courageous, daring and exciting. The initial chemistry, whether physical, intellectual or emotional, is enough to draw you into a state of frenzy about whether you've done the right thing or not. Your home is a reflection of you, and it may be that you've allowed someone into your space without thinking through the consequences.

However, be prepared to enjoy and delight, rather than panic. The following Feng Shui pre-romance enhancements will help you to relax, and improve your chances of a successful evening, whatever the outcome.

You may have already found out your chosen romantic's birth element and animal sign, and this will tell you the type of energy you are inviting into your home and whether it will balance with your own. Check the compatibility guide on page 54 to see your own ratings.

Harmonizing the Home

Entertaining for romantic evenings begins with getting the home in order. Depending on your birth element harmonize your home with a selection of the following Feng Shui tips to maximize your own personal happiness.

Checklist:

- Lighting
- Colour
- Mood setters

Lighting

IF YOU'RE FIRE Always avoid bright glaring light. Overhead lights are not conducive to good romance, and can bring a heavy centre of energy to the room in which you are entertaining. Go for table lamps and bright uplighters with dramatic shades and unusual colours, save the bright lights for the bathroom where your Fire nature can still be accessed.

IF YOU'RE EARTH Bring the lights down to almost floor level if you can. Place table lamps on the floor, candles on the fireplace, and if you're lucky enough to have an open fire and the weather is right, burn some logs. Use halogen bulbs and table lamps in the kitchen to highlight your nurturing and yet quietly erotic energy.

IF YOU'RE METAL Don't let the sparks fly too soon: tone down the need for precise areas of lighting. Be generous with small night-lights placed in groups around the room, at around waist height. If you like uplighters, place them in corners of the room, particularly if they can be hidden and mysterious, rather than bold and stark.

IF YOU'RE WATER Use lights that have low-wattage bulbs, or wall sconces with real candles. Place glass bowls of water under table lamps and sprinkle with glitter. Place three white candles in front of a mirror and let the whole room shimmer with reflections.

IF YOU'RE WOOD Find unusual lamp stands, or place pieces of gnarled wood or leather-bound books under the soft light of study lamps or library wall lights. If you prefer simple and unextravagant lighting, choose lights which can be changed with the flow of the evening, either hanging down over your dinner table, or on adjustable pendants.

Colour

IF YOU'RE FIRE Don't play up your own fiery nature with too much colour. Temper and harmonize your impulsive spirit and desire with a sense of earthy hues in your home. This could be simply a selection of terracotta jugs, peach and lemon-coloured lampshades or cushions, silk scarves or throws in warm autumnal russets and muted amber shades.

IF YOU'RE EARTH Balance your sensual nature with a touch of fire and brimstone! Use reds, shocking pinks or crimson in your fabrics or cushions. If you don't want to change your colour scheme, then just add a dash of fieriness with a print of poppies, sunflowers or a red sunset. Use mirrors and red candles on your mantelpiece or side table.

IF YOU'RE METAL Harmonize your integrity with the colours of the sea. Use aquamarine silk, or hang paintings or prints with a touch of deep blues and violets. If you're not fond of blues, then just choose a small piece of blue glass filled with tiny shells or beach stones, and place near the entrance to your home.

IF YOU'RE WATER Ensure you keep your deeper feelings balanced by bringing some silver, gold and white into your room. Use gilt-framed pictures or photos, fake silver or gold *objets d'art*, or fabrics and tapestries with fine gold threads thrown across your chairs. White can be used freely, but avoid stark white napkins and matching tablecloth – sure to create edginess rather than romance.

IF YOU'RE WOOD Balance your open and altruistic nature with fiery self-awareness. Use a touch of bright vibrant colour – reds, yellows, oranges – in your decor, or glossy paint and spiky brash flowers or *objets d'art*. If you loathe bright colours, then hang a string of red chilli peppers on your kitchen door. A touch of red here will do wonders to warm you as you entertain.

Romantic Mood Setters

IF YOU'RE FIRE Romance for Fire people is always a very special experience. To really indulge in your own potent and inspiring energy, ensure you have two red candles placed on a window ledge where their light will be reflected in the window glass, and also in a suitably placed mirror, perhaps on the wall opposite the window. This energizes your Fire nature and sets the mood for sparkling romance.

IF YOU'RE EARTH Sensual pleasure is what counts for Earth romantics, so get in touch with your own tactile senses by ensuring the whole room and home exudes fragrances that are warm, exotic and tantalizing. Use aromatherapy oils or scented candles, incense cones or sticks. Whatever your own personal choice of scents, dab some on the tablecloth, under the table, on sofas and chairs.

IF YOU'RE METAL Aesthetics and responsive communication are important for Metal, so ensure you bring gold and silver into your environment for added intensity of focus. Use the beauty of two gold- or silver-coloured candles in glass candlesticks and place them in the centre of the table, or use strong aluminium and steel furniture, as long as it has rounded edges. If you can't afford the luxury of such items, simply hang gold and silver threads from your windows to look like sparkling rain to ensure your magnetic charisma is revitalized.

IF YOU'RE WATER You are a born romantic and the joy of the unpredictable is what counts, so ensure you energize the mood with your own vital energy. Place a selection of shells and old pebbles found on a beach or images of the sea in the entrance to your home. A piece of amber placed carefully on a window ledge in the moonlight will ensure your evening is as charming and romantic as you could wish.

IF YOU'RE WOOD Sophisticated and unpossessive, you need to set a mood where you feel free and detached. Intellectual rapport is more important than chemistry. Find a favourite sculpture made of wood, if you have one – a wooden bird is excellent to bring a social and liberated atmosphere to your surroundings. Place this near to where you are going to eat, drink and be merry.

Important Bagua Locations

Draw a rough plan of your home, and the room in which you are going to entertain. Copy the Bagua map as in the diagram below to see where in your home the areas that are appropriate to you are located. Note that the area of the Bagua called Flow always falls in line with the wall in which is the main entrance to your home, and the main doorway to the specific room.

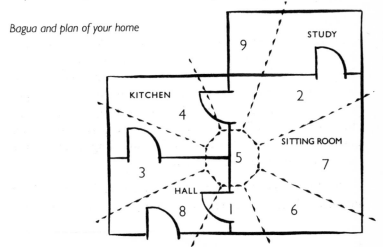

Bagua and plan of your home

For All Elements

Whatever element you are it is important to enhance the core of your home.

In the Connections area of your home (usually the centre of the house or room), well in advance of your guest's arrival, burn some favourite exotic incense to purify and enhance the inner movement of energy through this highly magical and invisible energy centre.

IF YOU'RE FIRE Disclosure is the area to enhance. If you can, find a prism for maximum refraction of light and place on a low table or window ledge in this area.

IF YOU'RE EARTH Tolerance is the area to enhance. If possible place a single piece of lapis lazuli on a window ledge or shelf in this area. If you can't get hold of lapis paint a pebble dark blue and gold and use it instead.

IF YOU'RE METAL Friendship is the area to enhance. Place a single white candle in a silver, gold or metal candlestick in this area. Light it before your visitor arrives.

IF YOU'RE WATER Flow is the area to enhance. Hang a painting of sensual or erotic art in this area. If you haven't time to find one you like, use fantasy images or surreal prints.

IF YOU'RE WOOD Initiative is the area to enhance. Place two yellow candles in wooden holders on a table in this area and place a scroll of handmade paper with a secret message in front of the candles.

Energizing You

IF YOU'RE FIRE Wear carnelian, bloodstone or dazzling red stones to enhance your passion and exuberance.

IF YOU'RE EARTH Choose smoky quartz or moonstones, wear close to your skin to channel your natural serenity.

IF YOU'RE METAL Diamonds are best if you can afford one! If not, wear white quartz crystal to radiate your erotic energy.

IF YOU'RE WATER Amber encourages self-worth and self-belief, so wear close to your heart to energize your integrity.

IF YOU'RE WOOD Wear verdelite, also known as green tourmaline, to inspire and energize your natural poise and sophistication.

NOW YOU'RE READY!

THE PLEASURES OF LOVE

Seduction

The art of seduction depends totally on how much someone else wants to be seduced! So be wise first and make sure you know what the chances and the consequences are.

IF YOUR CHOSEN SEDUCEE IS FIRE
Fire usually prefers to be the seducer, but may also enjoy being chased and the kind of games that can lead to passion. Keep the entertainment moving fast and impulsively, and you may succeed.

FENG SHUI TIPS
- Keep the room uncluttered, with an air of decadence and luxury.
- Bring in rich colours, fabrics and candles to make them feel at home, and ensure they are facing south or east when sitting at the table.

- Fire people respond well to simple food, aperitifs and first courses, or just one course rather than a feast.

- Food is not high on their list of priorities, so make sure you seduce with candles and wine, rather than wasting your time with haute cuisine, souffles, and hours spent slaving in the kitchen.

- You may succeed more easily in your adventure with a wilder approach to entertaining. Take the table out of the house and sit in the rain and wind, or surprise them by laying the table for a ten-course dinner and then only giving them champagne and pistachios.

- Fire people love to be shocked and to be daring, so if you're convinced they are as attracted to you as you to them, play strip snap.

IF THEY'RE EARTH

Can take ages to be seduced. Usually reserved and cautious about what they eat and drink, but when they flip into sensual gear, you'll probably be the one who is seduced by their extraordinary erotic nature.

FENG SHUI TIPS

- Earth people love their food, their drink and their bodies. If you excel at cooking then show off and be flamboyant about your wares.

- Offer them plenty of nibbles before the meal, as they get nervous and introspective if you show any signs of ambivalence.

- Seduce with warm lighting, an open fire if you have one, plenty of soft sofas and deep piled rugs or carpets. Sit them facing south-west or north-east.

- Suggest they take their shoes off when they enter your home – it may be your new-found way of being close to nature or just a temporary indulgence, but Earth people usually respond well to the touch of different textures beneath their toes.

- Unusual cuisine will tempt them closer into touching you.
- Sensuality is Earth's keyword. Choose food like asparagus, pasta, clear soup spiked with brandy, champagne crepes, or Chinese noodles. Sensual food is not about chewing, it's about tasting and tonguing.

IF THEY'RE METAL

Difficult to get close to, unless you keep your own cool distance. This could be a very intense kind of seduction, but if you persist the results can be out of this world and totally compelling.

FENG SHUI TIPS

- Metal people are discriminating and discreet, so make sure the food you serve is sophisticated, minimal and to the point. Crisp, cool, elegant and organic foods are more likely to be appreciated than rich sugary deserts.
- Make light conversation and keep the lights sparse but illuminating. Sit them facing west or north-west.
- Choose wines carefully, in fact keep a stock of different ones just in case your Metal guest has deliberately awkward taste. If you can't stretch to a wine cellar, suggest they bring their favourite.
- Always give Metal seducees a view of the door or entrance. They hate to feel vulnerable, and if you add security to their visit, they may relax long enough to enjoy it.
- Keep the decor simple and don't go crazy with too many candles or you may find your seducee starts blowing them out.
- Ensure your napkins are scrupulously clean, and you've checked that your Metal guest isn't a strict vegetarian. They often are.

IF THEY'RE WATER

Carefree and beguiling, they will try to escape quickly if cornered. Take care with Water, you never really know where you are with them, so avoid obvious flaunting. They thrive on more dangerous arts, like highly suggestive conversation, rather than actual physical contact.

FENG SHUI TIPS

- Relax Water people with nibbles, and fine wine or cocktails as soon as they enter. Ensure they sit at the table facing north or south.

- Irresistible scents of cooking, for example, garlic, rosemary, basil, fresh limes, induce a mysterious quality which Water finds enchanting.

- Romance is the evocative delights of music, wine, candlelight and flowing water. Bubbling aquariums or the sound of the sea can seduce them into staying for a while.

- Suggest green tea as a possible accompaniment to the meal. Use proper oriental teapots and bowls, and take turns to sip the tea. Water likes this kind of subtle suggestion.

- Place a crystal ball in the centre of the table and offer to tell their future. The crystal itself will energize their own romantic imagination which is incomparable!

- Food can be anything you like. Water is adaptable, but they won't eat heavy meals.

IF THEY'RE WOOD

Use intellectual wit and sophisticated language, fashion, art, any topic under the sun and you may enter their space more easily than by physical suggestion. Wood people won't be seduced easily and prefer to do the seducing, particularly if they believe they are doing so!

- Wood people need to feel free and under no obligation. So keep the lights undimmed, the music sophisticated, and the conversation ambiguous.

- Ensure Wood seducees face east or south-east.

- Food can be a major dilemma for Wood, either they'll eat anything or nothing. However, they are always ready to experiment, so try the latest fashion in cuisine and the most outrageous aperitif.

- Sofas are not beneficial for intellectual romance. Always keep the conversation going across the dinner table, and finish with champagne or the best brandy (if you can't afford it, go to the other extreme and buy homemade country wines and be truly bohemian).

- Have a painting, photo or sculpture that draws attention to itself. Highly engaging for Wood, and may keep them staying longer than you expect.

- Place a piece of malachite on your window ledge or sideboard. The intensity of its energy adds charisma to any seduction technique.

Proposals

This is not just about marriage proposals, but can mean proposing to take a holiday together, a weekend or simply forming a relationship. If you are nervous about your question and unsure of the response from your partner or possible partner, then by entertaining at home you can at least ensure you are off to a good start. For 'out of home' Feng Shui tips see the section further on in this chapter.

'Come round for a drink?'

Always make sure you have energized yourself according to your element as suggested at the beginning of this chapter.

Good communication also means enhancing the right areas of the room, and ensuring you are placed in the most auspicious seat or part of the room for your proposal.

With your Bagua plan over the room in which you are intending to make your offer or proposal, find the area which corresponds to being cool. This is the area of invisible energy which can vitalize and harmonize your ability to give and take, to put forward ideas and to do so with openness and ease. It will also give others the opportunity to relax and take in what you are saying without judgement or feelings of over-commitment.

Place a single bowl of exotic fruits, like passion fruit, pomegranates, peaches, lychees, figs, dark plums, in this area of your room to give pleasure to the energy of communication.

Ensure you are facing your most auspicious direction, and that your guest does not have their back to the doorway. Good Feng Shui is about your own placement as well as that of objects in the environment.

Auspicious directions for communication

FIRE – FACE NORTH
EARTH – FACE NORTH-WEST
METAL – FACE EAST
WATER – FACE SOUTH
WOOD – FACE WEST

A Romantic Dinner For Two – at Home

Here is a suggestion for a complete romantic dinner for two with all the accoutrements. Whatever element you are, it goes without saying that you should bring in the auspicious enhancements that have already been suggested for you earlier in the chapter.

The table

If possible choose a round table, curves are always more auspicious than sharp-edged squares and oblongs. However, if you don't have the choice, place a good heavy tablecloth over the table and this will soften the lines.

Don't always assume you have to sit opposite each other. This can put a heavy emphasis on eye contact. Fine if you are both ready to gaze suggestively into each other's souls, but precarious if the romance has only just begun.

Sit diagonally next to each other (as in the diagram below), and preferably ensure your guest sits to your left and you have the support of the back wall behind you.

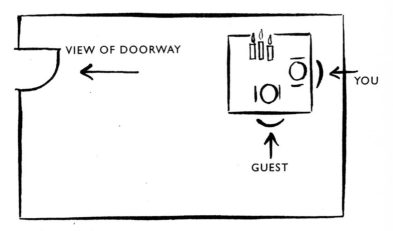

Seating arrangement for romance at home

The area behind you is where you are most vulnerable, and it must be firm, supportive and impenetrable, particularly in a romantic encounter, where you need to feel safe.

The setting

Use a red or dark-coloured tablecloth to evoke an atmosphere of sensuality and passion. Use at least three candles, preferably large church candles that will take a long time to burn, and place them in the centre of the table, if you are sitting next to each other, or at the side, if sitting opposite.

Take a glass bowl, fill it with water and sprinkle with rose petals or place small white flowers on the surface for grace and serenity. If you know your birth elements, place the corresponding crystals beneath the candle arrangement. This will emphasize your particular energy needs.

Glasses should be elegant, long-stemmed and preferably tapering at the top, rather than open.

Plates can be any colour, but bear in mind that patterned plates can create complicated energy and in turn confuse and distract the levels of good communication. Use plain colours if you can, and always eat your bread from the table top, not a side plate. Bread broken on the table shows respect for the food and the support which you are sharing together.

Down on the floor

This is the most auspicious place to begin your romantic evening. If you are both decked out in suits and stockings and the full romantic kit, then you may need to sit on sofas and chairs, but the whole point of getting down to ground level means you are more in tune with each other's vibrations. Down-to-earth levelling is auspicious for the balancing of dissimilar energies. It puts neither of you in a more powerful position, and allows the energy to circulate freely.

The drink

Always provide a selection of drinks – this is fairly obvious if you don't know someone – but to add some magic to the evening here are two special Feng Shui enhancers, one alcoholic, one non-alcoholic, both preferably taken while being romantic at floor level!

Pre-dinner

Place a sugar cube in the base of a large wine glass, add a squeeze of fresh lime juice, a good measure of brandy, and top up with dry sparkling wine or champagne. This is an extraordinary, powerful drink, so proceed with caution! Sit at a low table, or pile cushions on the floor near a coffee table, and serve with pistachios or stoned olives.

Alternatively

Offer your guest a romantic tea ceremony. Choose a low table and pile up some large cushions and sit on the floor. Choose an oriental teapot if you can and two small drinking bowls or cups without handles.

Use green tea rather than the black teas that we commonly buy. Green tea usually only comes from China and is not fermented like black teas. The best is called Dragon's Well tea or Lung Ching, and has the most beneficial properties. (You can get green teas in most supermarkets now, but special ones can be found in Chinese stores and supermarkets.) Dragon's Well tea is expensive, but is the most luscious and magical of them all. Yunnan green teas (Yunnan is an area of China) are also highly regarded, and are the strongest, most potent and energizing.

Whatever tea you choose, it is the art of pouring and sipping that is as much the key to harmony as the tea itself. Remember, don't let the tea stew too long, and sip it slowly while you watch each other's lips around the edge of the cup.

The food

For romantic dinners choose Yang foods as starters to stimulate and bring desire to the occasion. Follow with Yin foods to cool and bring realization and clarity to the romance, whether it's for keeps, or merely a short but sweet encounter.

Use one of these Yang foods in your first course or main dish: onions, walnuts, sunflower seeds, peanuts, smoked fish, red meat, chillies, garlic, eggs.

Use one of these Yin foods in your main course and/or pudding/desert: white fish, cucumber, spinach, tomatoes, shrimps or prawns, tofu (beancurd), broccoli, beer, cabbage, green beans, ice cream, strawberries, almonds, grapes.

As you may not know whether your guest is a predominantly Yin or Yang type of person, it's also important to include some neutral foods, as they do not disturb the balance of Yin and Yang in your own or your guest's body.

Choose from: bread, chicken, peas, beans, rice, peaches, pasta.

Specific Feng Shui enhancements

Once you've got your food and table prepared, add the following vitalizers to your home to ensure that romance is in the air.

In the kitchen – either place a small bowl of red chilli peppers beside your cooker or hang a garland of dried ones on the kitchen door for maximum passion.

In the hallway – place a single piece of rose quartz crystal near the doorway and touch it just before you open the door to your romantic guest, and every time you pass it by.

In the room in which you eat – have a small bowl or plate filled to the brim with stones, pebbles or small polished crystals to ground the romantic energy.

Finally, the bedroom – you may have no intention of either your guest or yourself entering this room, but it is important to ensure your most private of rooms is filled with grace.

Place a piece of jade, malachite or green tourmaline here for sophistication.

Lighting – romance thrives on atmospheric lighting. If you are able to incorporate uplighters, mood lighting, unusual lampshades and soft yellow, red and warm lights into your interior then do so. However, twenty candles grouped in front of the fireplace will provide infinitely more powerful energy than the most luxurious of electric lights.

A ROMANTIC DINNER FOR TWO – HOW TO SURVIVE IN A RESTAURANT

Like most of us the chances are your first romantic 'date' together will be on neutral ground. Here you will both feel free from the restraints of someone else's private life, and be surrounded by the atmosphere and mood of a restaurant meant to make you feel good.

Here are some Feng Shui tips for romantic meals in restaurants. Placing yourself in an auspicious way can mean the romance quickens or slows according to your personal intentions, rather than anyone else's!

In the diagram on the next page the layout of the restaurant shows you the most auspicious directions for seating.

Be Feng Shui wise and carry your own personal element crystal in your handbag or jacket. If the energy enhancement is with you, then you can feel secure that however unbalanced or inharmonious the environment, you have your own empowerment working with you.

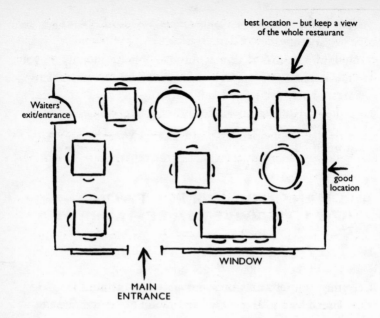

best location – but keep a view of the whole restaurant

Waiters' exit/entrance

good location

WINDOW

MAIN ENTRANCE

Checklist of element crystals:

FIRE – carnelian or bloodstone, ruby

EARTH – smoky quartz, tiger's eye or moonstone

METAL – diamond, white quartz crystal or obsidian

WATER – amber, turquoise or lapis lazuli

WOOD – malachite, green tourmaline or peridot

Getting Intimate

If you are beyond the stage of romance and fully engaged in passion and intimacy, then a meal can often be the true beginning of a night to remember. Choose soft blues and greens at the dinner table for simple suppers or meals. The chances are you'll be hungry for love, rather than food, and too much red, orange or brown can lead to stimulating appetites rather than desire!

106

The most important enhancements are those which bring your own energies into balance, so here's a sample of harmonizers and energizers for each combination of elements at the dinner table, assuming you already have the following ingredients:

Candlelight – at least one or two candles – for Fire energy

Wine or champagne or sparkling water for Water energy

Soft yellows, greens in tablecloths, napkins, crockery or cutlery for Wood energy

Cutlery, candlesticks or cruet made of metal, aluminium, stainless steel, silver, gold for Metal energy

A bowl or jug of fresh flowers/leaves/fruits for Earth energy.

METAL/METAL

Keep the lighting subdued and eat at a round or curved table. Use red candles on the window ledge or in front of a mirror to encourage fire into your relationship. Burn some patchouli incense after dinner and place a huge bowl of strawberries and raspberries soaked in vodka or champagne for a final temptation. The rest of the food will be irrelevant!

METAL/FIRE

Have a bowl of luscious fruit placed invitingly near the sofa or comfortable lounging area. Use mangoes, figs, apricots and melons, and suggest you peel each other's fruit across the dinner table. Place a piece of pink tourmaline or rose quartz near where you eat to ensure that you activate awareness for each other.

METAL/WOOD

To invite exuberant energy into your entertainment use citrus-scented incense or yellow and black candles, two or four in the middle of the table or beside your sofa. Find several mirrors and hang them facing the candlelight. To inspire and fuel your desire for starters place cool crisp foods on the table that require fingers rather than forks – celery sticks, cheese straws, pistachio nuts and olives.

METAL/EARTH

Bring red lighting, lamps or candles into your intimate entertainment. Drink red wine rather than white, or prepare a pudding of red fruits steeped in brandy. Place a piece of amber on your dinner table to draw away any negative energy, and for total involvement place a mirror on a wall that will reflect the sunrise.

METAL/WATER

Offer unusual teas – peppermint, green or vanilla flavours – steeped in small oriental pots. Serve crisp white wines, light vegetables, fresh salads and simple fish or meat across a rich dark tablecloth. Drink from deep-red glasses. Place a piece of amethyst on your window ledge where it can absorb the moonlight.

WATER/WATER

Use white tableware, silver candlesticks and gold candles. Keep the lighting subdued and have a corner that is darker, mysterious and unknown. Place a piece of carnelian or blood-stone in this corner for maximum passion. Music is a must, so is simple food and exquisite wine. To keep desire flowing, energize your room with images of dreams or fantasy.

WATER/FIRE

Play the sounds of a jungle at night to ground you both in each other's energy. Place a piece of jade or green tourmaline as a centrepiece on the table. Drink cold red burgundy (yes, chilled red wine), and eat salty, spicy foods with hints of the exotic. Finish with peeled grapes and then light black candles.

WATER/WOOD

Burn exotic aromatherapy oils before your visitor arrives. Energize your room with lapis lazuli placed on a window ledge, or beside two blue candles. Use gold and silver at the dinner table – either fake gold paper napkins, cutlery or glasses. Dine on golden-coloured foods, like brandy snaps and honey cakes, and dark champagne.

WATER/EARTH

This is one combination that responds to wind chimes. Keep the dinner table low, perhaps eat from the floor, or at a low coffee table, sit on cushions and feel the earth beneath you. Use plenty of candles scattered around the room at a higher level. Eat out of gold- or silver-coloured bowls, use chopsticks or fingers, use woks or simple fondues.

FIRE/FIRE

Start with a quick burst of Ravel's Bolero, then light white candles in the centre of your table, open some chilled champagne or Vin Mousseux, and nibble olives, nuts and croutons. Place a white quartz crystal on the window ledge or in front of a mirror for maximum passion.

FIRE/EARTH

Place a tall red candle and a smaller yellow candle in front of a window or mirror where the light will be reflected, to enhance your sensual awareness. Crystals like smoky quartz, or for maximum impact, onyx, are wonderful energizers for this combination. Choose tactile food – spaghetti, noodles and lashings of strawberries.

FIRE/WOOD

Make sure you create an atmosphere filled with the rich aromas of your meal. Dark, burnt coffee with cream, the swirl of brandy in polished glasses, sophisticated food that doesn't take long to eat or prepare. Make ice cubes out of champagne or sparkling wine and dribble brandy or your favourite liqueur over the ice. Place a white quartz crystal in the centre of the table with a single white candle for maximum illumination and instinctual awareness.

WOOD/WOOD

The dinner table can be as minimalist or as fussy as you like. Whatever style you prefer, go to an extreme! Use gold-coloured candles, metal candlesticks and exotic flowers overflowing a bowl or jug. Or remove all decoration and eat simple soups and bread, with jugs of wine and cheeses. Take the chairs outside if you can and eat beneath the stars, the wind and even the rain!

WOOD/EARTH

Play music or sounds of waterfalls, gurgling streams or rushing torrents. Place red and blue candles in the centre of your dinner table – red for inflaming passion, and blue for intrigue and mystery. Place a piece of amethyst on the window ledge for deep trust and integrity, and enjoy the pleasure of exotic fruits and aromatic wines.

EARTH/EARTH

Place a small piece of azurite in front of a mirror and light two red candles either side of it to clear away painful memories and to enjoy the present. Drink crisp white wines chilled for hours as an aperitif and then old clarets or oak-aged red. Enjoy a slow languorous meal and add spices and warmth to the occasion.

Bedroom Food

The delights of the bedroom can often be enhanced with food, whether it is breakfast in bed or a late-night supper with a bottle of champagne. Here are some ideas for harmonious entertaining in the bedroom:

Breakfast in bed

- Place a single white flower on the tray or table as a symbol of enthusiasm and happiness for the new day.
- Eat a selection of Yang food like peanut butter on toast or smoked kippers and eggs for a dynamic and stimulating day.
- Ensure you balance with green tea or mineral water rather than coffee, and as much fruit as you want which won't affect the balance of Yin and Yang.
- Place a single aromatherapy candle or incense stick on a window ledge or shelf to cleanse the atmosphere and rejuvenate you and the room.

Late-night feast

Drink champagne or a chilled white wine in an ice bucket. Two huge glasses to sip from and linger over. Use plates that have images of flowers like peonies, magnolias, lilies or poppies. The sexual qualities that these flowers were believed to have are transmitted to the food on the dish and then absorbed on eating – a quick way to feed your lover with erotic energy.

Delight in a selection of erotic foods like passion fruit, mangoes, apricots and strawberries, peaches. Alternatively choose from these favourite aphrodisiacs for each element:

Chocolate – Wood
Oysters – Metal
Stuffed vine leaves or figs – Fire
Honey on toast – Earth
Avocados – Earth
Creamed rice – Water
Caviar – Water
Bowls of king prawns – Metal

Ice cream – Wood
Pickled walnuts – Fire

Other tips

- Place a piece of rose quartz in your bedroom to activate harmony and love.

- For more passion and sensuality use patchouli or opium incense or oils or light black and red candles.

- Dab your sheets, clothes, and bed with perfumes and scents that you prefer.

- Place a selection of gourds in a wooden bowl on your window ledge. These are an ancient symbol of the combination of male and female, and will encourage a good flow of sexual energy.

- If you prefer to avoid alcohol, then have a late-night tea ceremony. For morning passion, place a piece of carnelian under your pillows or mattress while you sleep.

A NOTE ON BEING ENTERTAINED – FOR WOMEN ONLY!

There will be many times when you will be entertained or invited to someone else's party, so depending on your own birth element energy, here are some ideas for enhancing your charisma and success wherever and whoever's threshold you are crossing:

IF YOU ARE FIRE   Silk stockings are a must, particularly shimmering white ones. Wear beneath dresses that give a tantalizing glimpse of what's on offer. If you're feeling incredibly sexy make sure you wear deep blood-red or bitter-chocolate-coloured camisole tops or knickers. A glimpse of satin or a low-backed plunging little number will be enough to set the room alight.

Choose a bloodstone, or a deep ruby-coloured crystal on a choker to ensure that your impatient spirit is grounded enough to enflame the right kind of interest.

IF YOU ARE EARTH If you can bear the heat and you've got the figure, wear leather jeans or fake animal designs. You're an artist when it comes to sensuality, so make sure your body glows with awesomely scented oil beneath any of the tactile fabrics you use. Invest in the most expensive perfume you can to give you extra zest and to balance your sometimes cautious approach to company. If you want to remain cool and exude sex appeal more quietly then wear amber close to your heart. Use real lapis lazuli or fake sapphires to stun others with your focused reality.

IF YOU ARE METAL Your single-minded and ambitious passion can be enhanced with multi-pierced ears hung with tiny rings, or if you prefer, your fingers dripping with fine silver or gold. Use very dark make-up, coal blacks, charcoals, burnt metallics, and blushers with a hint of gold. Lipstick can be ruby red, or bitter brown, as long as it's dark and beguiling enough to express your volatile and extremist nature. If you're feeling particularly in need of self-empowerment then use an erotically placed false tattoo to raise a few eyebrows.

IF YOU ARE WATER Like a siren from the sea, leave your hair loose and flowing or pile with a coral hairpiece. Make use of your deeply seductive eyes and use ocean colours and kohl eyeliners. Tie aquamarine voiles, or silks the colour of rose quartz around your waist or hips, or swirl a fine muslin scarf around your neck like Isadora Duncan. Remember to take it off before you get in the car! To keep your romantic imagination grounded, make sure you use heady intoxicating perfumes in all the pulse places.

IF YOU ARE WOOD Emphasize that radical air of cool glamour with dramatic shapes, lines, or colours. For real Wood eccentricity, reveal your belly button and attach an opal or a stone like chalcedony at your naval. Keep to natural make-up, and drip seductive, girly perfumes along your main veins to balance your liberal style with a touch of hidden sexuality. As you warm up and your altruistic nature gets into full swing, sprinkle glitter-gel across your chest like a stream of twinkling stars.

Crystals and semi-precious stones are excellent enhancements. Make sure you're wearing the one related to your birth element for that extra magic!

IF YOUR BIRTH ELEMENT IS FIRE Fire connects to active, exuberant and dynamic energy. You are optimistic and daring. Enhance and harmonize your fun-loving heart by wearing carnelian, bloodstone or garnet.

IF YOUR BIRTH ELEMENT IS EARTH Earth connects to sensual, receptive and seductive energy. You are consistent in your desires. Energize your self-awareness by wearing malachite, lapis lazuli or smoky quartz.

IF YOUR BIRTH ELEMENT IS METAL Metal connects to determined, ambitious and erotic energy. You are dedicated to success in everything. Empower your integrity by wearing a single diamond, selenite or a white quartz crystal.

IF YOUR BIRTH ELEMENT IS WATER Water connects to sensitive, flowing and elusive energy. You are romantic and often unpredictable. To energize your intuitive feelings wear amethyst, fluorite or amber.

IF YOUR BIRTH ELEMENT IS WOOD Wood connects to sophisticated, glamorous and poised energy. You are everyone's friend and need to feel free. Enhance your altruistic nature by wearing turquoise, chalcedony or green tourmaline.

CHAPTER FIVE

Entertaining Alfresco and Celebration Parties

Every season brings with it different reasons or moods for entertaining outside, particularly if you are in a temperate climate where the changes are most marked.

OUTDOOR FENG SHUI ENHANCEMENTS FOR WINTER

Hang wind chimes in the trees near your house, but make sure they are weatherproof!

OUTDOOR FENG SHUI ENHANCEMENTS FOR AUTUMN

Place a wooden bowl of figs, pomegranates or avocado pears beneath your favourite tree or deciduous bush.

OUTDOOR FENG SHUI ENHANCEMENTS FOR SPRING

Take a dozen tiny terracotta pots and fill each with one spring flower of your choice, then group together near the main entrance door.

OUTDOOR FENG SHUI ENHANCEMENTS FOR SUMMER

Hang bells, rather than wind chimes, in your trees. Good Feng Shui means ensuring that the area outside your home is beneficial to both the flow of ch'i around your house, as well as your own personal energy.

To the front of your house, usually just outside your front door, is an area that is highly auspicious and known by the Chinese as the 'Red Bird'. Make sure you keep this area uncluttered and that any plants, paths or steps are clear so that the energy can move freely.

Red Bird area

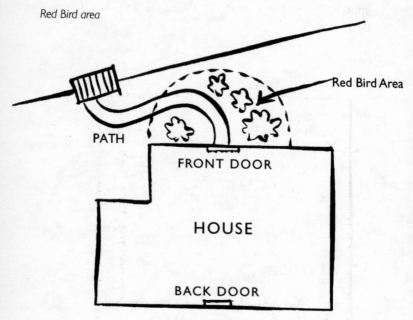

USING THE BAGUA OUTSIDE

To maximize the success of your outdoor party, ensure you use the Bagua to work out which areas of the garden or outdoor area are auspicious for enjoyment and harmony.

In the example opposite, the bottom edge of the Bagua, Water, is placed in line with the wall that has the exit from the house. Thus, the Fire area is at the furthest end of the garden.

The most auspicious areas of the Bagua for outside parties are Friendship and Pleasure, so ensure you place the following Feng Shui remedies in one of these areas depending on which elemental energy is dominant in your home. (If you are Fire and your partner is Earth, then use the elemental remedy which corresponds to whoever will do most of the organization. Usually you!)

Bagua in the garden

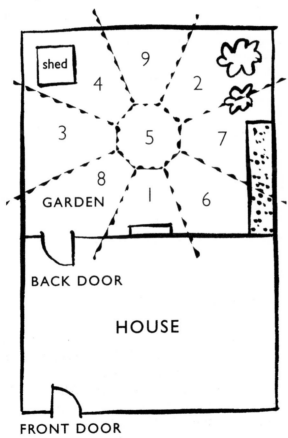

FRIENDSHIP OR PLEASURE

IF YOUR DOMINANT ELEMENT IS FIRE: Place red flowers, plants with tall spiky leaves, even cacti in summer.

IF YOUR DOMINANT ELEMENT IS EARTH: Place hanging lanterns, or standing storm lamps, white flowering plants in pots.

IF YOUR DOMINANT ELEMENT IS METAL: Place two huge urns or stoneware cider jars, dark blue flowers or grasses.

IF YOUR DOMINANT ELEMENT IS WATER: A miniature fountain, or small water feature, if not available, plenty of blue and green pots.

IF YOUR DOMINANT ELEMENT IS WOOD: A beautiful wooden or metal bench or chair, or a wooden wheelbarrow.

PRE-GUEST RITUALS FOR CLEARING THE OUTSIDE OF DIFFICULT ENERGY

Gardens may seem restful places where the world does not intrude (if you are lucky), and yet even the most peaceful of outer worlds still needs energizing before your guests arrive. If you live in the town centre and have the noise and fume pollution to contend with as well, then ensure you use the extra cures recommended here.

Light some large garden candles or flames the day before the party, sprinkle with your favourite exotic oils or with herbs while they burn to cleanse and purify the garden area. Although you may still hear the noise of the traffic, and find the birds have left you new messages on the bench, you will have given your space or your garden the benefit of clearing energy.

The night before place a piece of amber in the centre of your garden or space, cover with a terracotta pot or dish and it will draw in any remaining negative energy. Wash the amber the following morning in mineral water, or the sea if you happen to live near enough!

In the morning of the party hang a set of wooden or shell wind chimes from a tree branch in the sunlight (if you don't have any trees just hang them from an outside hook or nail near your back door). This will help to disperse the difficult energy during the day.

Lastly, place a grouping of red flowering plants near your main entrance to the garden. This increases Fire, Earth and Wood energy which are needed to stimulate and activate the atmosphere of your party.

WHAT TO USE OUTSIDE

Metal furniture is currently in fashion outside in our gardens, so ensure you balance this powerful energy with plenty of Water enhancements.

Water balancer for Metal furniture: take a large stone sink filled with water or a tiny pond (use a big plastic box, and line with black plastic) and place flowers and floating candles on the surface.

Wood furniture may be your chosen outdoor medium, and if this is the case it must be balanced with Fire energizers, as the whole garden will be heavy on wood (plants, trees, fences, trellis, etc.).

Fire balancer for Wood furniture: hang storm lanterns in the trees, or place a line of lamps down the side of your drive or entrance to the main entertaining area.

Water features are now common in small and large gardens. However, although it is highly auspicious to have ponds, waterfalls or fountains near your house, it is equally important to make sure they are not stagnant, and that the water is in constant flow. This is good energy to have near you, but you must remember to balance it with Wood. Too much emphasis on Water will make for jittery guests and confused relationships.

Wood balancer for too many Water features: use stone or wooden statues of people, animals or abstract images. Place near the water where their shadows can be reflected on the surface.

NIGHT-TIME ALFRESCO

Daytime parties outside are usually barbecues and buffets held in summer, but night-time alfresco entertainment can be held at any time from winter celebrations with fireworks, to a supper party on a hot night with the mosquitos biting.

For SUMMER nights and supper parties use the following energizer to instil fluidity and flexibility into the hot sticky night. *Energizer:* use water features, either a fountain or miniature waterfall, or even small stone or terracotta bowls of water sprinkled with rosemary, thyme or mint.

For cold WINTER nights with bonfires, fireworks and hot food, hang lights through your favourite tree, or use outdoor candles and light as many as you can to bring a generous warmth and glow to the cold weather.

DAYTIME ALFRESCO

To make the most of your daytime party use the following enhancement for exuberant guests. Remember, colour is as important outside as it is inside.

If your garden predominantly faces east, use balloons, tableware and napkins in shades of green and yellow. Place the table or serving bench in the shade and decorate the table with natural art, like wooden sculpture, gnarled branches and wooden bowls of gourds or seasonal fruits.

If your garden predominantly faces west, use silver or gold napkins and white tablecloths, metal salt and pepper sets, aluminium cutlery or water jugs, spiky decorations of wrought-iron sconces filled with white lilies, or any white flowers in season, threaded through the metal rungs.

If your garden predominantly faces south, use reds, oranges and bright vibrant colours for your tableware. Ensure you have cascades of flowers in jugs (whatever is in season) in rich colours to stimulate the appetite. Decorate outside tables with red candles in the winter and in the summer use red glasses, or hang mirrors in the trees or bushes.

If your garden predominantly faces north, then choose subtle blues, sky colours, greys and violets. Use a water decoration, a miniature waterfall, or paint a huge water scene on your back wall or fence in rich blues and blacks, but make sure it depicts flowing water. Provide plenty of vessels filled with water and place around your garden, and sprinkle with silver glitter or white flower petals.

THE GUESTS

Outdoor parties don't always mean your guests remain outside, particularly if the weather changes! Hang a set of wind chimes near the main entrance through which your guests come and go. These will help to disperse and circulate all the energy and ensure that whoever passes by carries only beneficial energy into the home, and negative energy out from it.

FOOD AND DRINK

Obviously, it is common sense to use hot food on a cold night and cold food on a hot day. However, choose one or two foods from these nourishing and neutral foods as they can be used in large quantities without disturbing the balance of Yin and Yang.

Bread	Garlic
Rice	Fish
Chicken	Spinach
Carrots	Olive oil

DRINK

For summer parties choose from chilled white wines, champagne and sparkling wines, Buck's Fizz, if it's early in the day, or a lavish but dry punch filled with fruit and ice cubes. For winter or night-time parties, red wines, mulled wine, beers, and chocolate and coffee are excellent balancers.

BIG CELEBRATION PARTIES

Preparing your Home

First you need to know which is the most auspicious direction for your own home. Look at the diagram below to see how.

Layout of table/room for buffet party

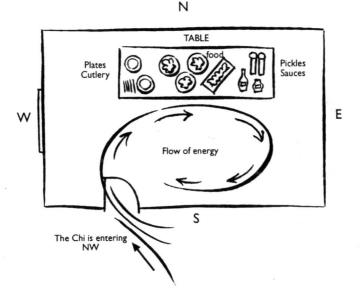

Whichever direction the ch'i is entering your house is the home's most auspicious direction.

IF IT IS PREDOMINANTLY SOUTH — place at least five red candles in metal candlesticks in the southern side of your entertaining room, and ensure you have a reasonable-sized mirror in this room to increase the auspicious energy. You don't need to light the candles, but make sure they are in a close group.

IF IT IS PREDOMINANTLY NORTH – a fish tank may not be a viable acquisition for your home, but if you do have one always make sure the fish have a filter whether coldwater or exotic. Don't use a goldfish in a bowl! If you haven't any interest in aquariums then simply take a large blue jug of any blue flowers in season and place them in the north side of your entertaining room.

IF IT IS PREDOMINANTLY EAST – place a pile of books on a side table in the east side of your room. To reinforce the energy either make an arrangement of gnarled wood branches, or interesting-shaped sculptural plants, and place beside the pile of books.

IF IT IS PREDOMINANTLY WEST – place a glass bowl or vase of white lilies in the west side of your entertaining room, and beside the flower arrangement stand a metal figure or sculpture, the more abstract the better, either in bronze, steel, wrought iron or even fake gold, or silver. If you don't have one, then find a brass utensil or object and place it there instead.

WEDDING PARTIES

For wedding parties and receptions, it is essential to work with the elemental energies of the bride and groom rather than worry about anyone else.

Find out their birth element by looking it up in the chart at the beginning of this book.

METAL/METAL WEDDING

Energy has to move freely for these two, so hang floaty muslin curtains or drapes in an appropriate window. Use plenty of red and white candles, or light patchouli and jasmine incense just before the guests arrive. Place flowers that have a calming and sensual energy, like camellias, magnolias and cream roses.

Place a piece of coral in a secret location to activate affection and dedication.

METAL/FIRE WEDDING

Place at least five large bowls of exotic fruit around the room. Use luscious, sensual fruits like apricots, pomegranates, peaches, mangoes and plums. Place a piece of pink tourmaline or rose quartz on a window ledge where it can glisten in the sunlight, or if it is an evening party, near a good light source for dynamic passion and a long and successful marriage.

METAL/WOOD WEDDING

Ensure that on your wedding table you have finger bowls of water for each guests, preferably in small glass or blue porcelain bowls. Float white or blue flower petals on the surface of the water, or whole flowers without stems. Place a piece of carnelian on a mantelpiece or high shelf, well away from the energies at floor level. This will inspire awareness and a successful partnership.

METAL/EARTH WEDDING

Place some scented candles along the window sills, particularly those with strong erotic perfumes like cinabar, opium, sandalwood or patchouli. This will stimulate and generate the flow of energy before your guests arrive. If you find it too overpowering for a wedding party, blow them out just before. Use a mixture of blues and reds for your flower arrangements, and a piece of amber near the entrance door to dispel any negative energy that comes in with your guests. Colours should be bold and vibrant – don't use pastels.

METAL/WATER WEDDING

Ensure the scheme for tablecloths, decoration and flower arrangements incorporates soft colours like pistachio, peppermint, almond blossom, lavender or cornflower blue. Use billowing voile and silk curtains at the main doorway and strong, tall, growing upright plants around all areas of the room. Finally place a piece of azurite near, or on, the wedding table to clear away old memories and refresh and inspire the new beginning.

WATER/WATER WEDDING

Use unusual lighting at night, or hang paper blinds or muslin in the window if it is a daytime wedding party. Find a beautiful wooden carving or sculpture, as big and as extravagant in style as possible, and use it as a base for an arrangement with a mass of green foliage plants. Bring red flowers into your arrangements, or place red candles in front of mirrors or on window ledges for potency and enlivening mutual happiness.

WATER/FIRE WEDDING

Use strong terracotta-coloured bowls, sage-green glasses, and ochre candles. If you aren't fond of these colours then use plenty of greens and autumnal hues in your flower arrangements. For inspiration and a successful partnership place a small piece of jade or smoky quartz in two velvet bags and position them together in front of a large mirror. When the couple are about to leave give them as good-luck talismans.

WATER/WOOD WEDDING

Paint stars on the ceiling of your venue in silver or gold paint, especially if you are having an evening occasion. If daytime, sprinkle tiny glittering stars onto a large bowl of water and place floating candles in the centre. Try to avoid metal furniture at this wedding celebration. Light blue and green candles for maximum pleasure, and for long-term happiness place a piece of green tourmaline on a window ledge or shelf.

WATER/EARTH WEDDING

Choose earth metals, gold, silver, bronze, copper, and wrought iron, for lighting and decoration. A bronze-effect chandelier would make a good centrepiece or place pewter goblets on the wedding table. Otherwise use a huge piece of white quartz crystal as a centrepiece surrounded by your favourite flowers. For genuine long-term happiness, ensure that you light lots of white, silver- or gold-coloured candles, whether it is a day or night-time event, and ask the happy couple to blow them out together as they make a wish.

FIRE/FIRE WEDDING

Take several glass bowls filled with water and place shells and coloured pieces of glass, marbles or crystals into the water to vitalize flexibility and sensitivity. Hang mirrors around the room to enrich the warmth and vibrancy of the occasion. Decorate your flower arrangements with gold or silver threads, ribbons or bows, for financial and emotional prosperity.

FIRE/EARTH WEDDING

Choose stainless-steel, bronze or silver candlesticks and yellow candles. If you have a candelabra hang gold threads or silver chains from the supports. Bring rich reds into your decor with huge blossoms or large paintings filled with fiery colours.

Place a piece of onyx on a window ledge to ground and stabilize the energy. Hang voile or muslin fabric across the wedding tables.

FIRE/WOOD WEDDING

Use wine coolers and ice buckets placed around the room, and make your ice cubes out of champagne. Place several white quartz crystals in the window so that the sunlight reflects on their surface. Use soft colours in your table scheme – creams, pastels, gentle yellows or faded ochres. Bring plants to the centrepiece rather than flowers, huge foliage arrangements rather than pretty cascades.

WOOD/WOOD WEDDING

Hang a gilt-framed mirror or painting in a prime position of the venue to maximize sophisticated energy. Use gold fabrics, silver-coloured wind chimes in an open window, and if you can obtain one, an indoor fountain or miniature waterfall. Place a piece of rose quartz in front of the huge mirror or painting for happiness and success.

WOOD/EARTH WEDDING

Use coloured wine glasses, preferably blues or reds, inky, misty colours rather than opaque. Place a collection of shells, stones, pebbles from the beach or corals on a window ledge or mantel-shelf, and beside this arrangement burn some incense, either pine or sandalwood, before the guests arrive. Place pine-nuts in small earthenware bowls on the wedding-feast table, and ensure you have a piece of amethyst near your entrance to enhance the awareness of one another's needs and values.

EARTH/EARTH WEDDING

Inspire passion with red tablecloths, red napkins, and red glasses for the table setting. Use deep-red or rich purple velvet cushions on old antique chairs. Use an indoor waterfall or fountain surrounded by luscious plants and huge stones or rocks. A bonsai tree would be invaluable for good luck and prosperity for the future. Place a piece of azurite on the wedding table to clear away the past and look forward to the future.

CHAPTER SIX

Five Stylish Dinner-Party Occasions

There are times when we want to celebrate or entertain for specific reasons. These five different examples are based on the five elemental energies which are so important in balancing and harmonizing your environment.

The element of Fire concerns progress, achievement, recognition and often fame. If you want to improve your own chances of success in any enterprise or if you want to impress, promote others or ensure your friends know about your future plans, then choose the INSPIRING dinner party.

The element of Earth concerns families, education, material needs and contentment. If you are planning a family get-together, a celebration of someone's birthday, exam pass or a quiet homely evening of indulgence, then choose the WARMING dinner party.

The element of Metal concerns autonomy, power and dedication. If you need to make crucial choices, debate decisions, articulate new ideas or celebrate financial rewards then choose the CRYSTAL dinner party.

The element of Water concerns communication and the imagination. It also relates to new beginnings and career changes. If you are celebrating a new job, a change of direction career-wise or moving house, announcing a marriage or an artistic success, then choose the MAGIC dinner party.

The element of Wood concerns friendship, diplomacy, health and aspirations. It relates to expanding new ideas, crossing different thresholds and expressing hopes and ideas to those who may not normally be open to change. If you are hoping for good news, or supporting changes in other people's lives, celebrating their good luck rather than your own, then choose the DRAGON dinner party.

Each of these dinner parties are designed for six people (apart from the CRYSTAL party which is particularly auspicious for five people), but obviously you may be inviting only three, four, eight or more. Don't try to use these dinner parties with more than ten people, as the energy balancing will become too complicated.

THE INSPIRING DINNER PARTY

The layout suggested below shows you how to set out the INSPIRING dinner party for six people. Notice that the Fire energy is concentrated at the far end of the room, rather than on the table, as this could be too overpowering for the guests.

FIRE ENHANCEMENTS
on side table here or here

Leave table clear at end and
centre except for one candle

Octagonal
mirrors
for guests

Who To Invite?

For a Fire party, try to invite ONE from the first group, and ONE from the second group. The first group will reinforce the Fire energy, the second group will generate energy, but also balance and soften any excess of mood. Avoid people from the last group, as they energize other occasions, but are not so suitable for the purposes of this dinner party.

GROUP ONE	GROUP TWO	GROUP THREE
Fire Horse	Earth Monkey	Water Rabbit
Wood Horse	Wood Dog	Metal Pig
Fire Dragon	Wood Monkey	Water Ox
Wood Dragon	Wood Horse	Metal Rooster
Fire Tiger	Earth Horse	Water Pig
Wood Tiger	Earth Dragon	Water Rooster
Fire Rat	Earth Rat	Metal Snake
Wood Rat	Earth Dog	Water Snake

NB: If your own element or animal sign falls into the latter category, then use a Feng Shui remedy: A piece of lapis lazuli placed in the kitchen, also a piece of white quartz crystal in the hallway.

Finally, if you can't ensure you have the right animal/element combination, then just work with the elements. Try to invite Wood, Fire and Earth friends.

Each of the invited guests can be placed in a certain position at the table according to their element. However, if you don't know their birth dates and can't look up their element, work only with your own element and that of your partner, colleague or close friend. Always make sure if you are Fire that you sit at the end of the table opposite to the concentration of Fire energy as in the above diagram.

For other element hosts:

IF YOU ARE EARTH sit in the seat which is to the left of the Fire energizers.

IF YOU ARE METAL sit in the seat which is nearest the Fire energizer.

IF YOU ARE WATER sit in the seat which is furthest away from the Fire energizer.

IF YOU ARE WOOD sit in the seat which is to the right of the Fire energizer.

If you find out all your guests overload the Fire energy, then you may need to bring in some Water energizer to put a damper on the possibility of creating too intense a friction! For example, if you have four Fire and two Wood guests, then use the following Water enhancement: Water balancer – use blue glass on the table.

The Preparation

Place three red candles in a group together on a red or yellow tablecloth on a side table. Light the candles well in advance of the dinner for at least half an hour to increase the Fire energy into your room.

Red is obviously going to be the major theme of an INSPIRING dinner party, and therefore it is most appropriate to bring red napkins, tablecloths and red flowers to the occasion. If you have any red paintings, sunsets, or images of stars, place these in your entertaining room.

As in the layout diagram, don't place any of your Fire objects in the centre of the table – this is one meal where you want to leave the core area open to receiving and regenerating the energy that Fire brings with it.

For each guest place a finger bowl beside their place setting, and drop some red petals on to the surface of the water, just before they arrive. This will balance the potent Fire energy.

Other Enhancements

Near the main entrance, and the one through which your guests will enter, place a bowl of red fruits, or a garland of red berries.

At the far end of your room, beside the candle setting, place three earthenware or terracotta bowls which contain in the first, pistachio nuts, in the second, black olives and in the third, green olives. All these add a balancing of Earth energizers, and you can also eat them!

As lighting is such a Fire energizer, incorporate vibrant lighting near the entrance to the room, and soft subdued lighting in two other corners. Light the candles on your Fire reinforcement table before beginning the meal, but if you want specific light over the table then choose or adapt from the following: If you have an overhead light that is not too intense then simply use this, but make sure that the table is centrally placed beneath. Or place one cream-coloured or church-type candle in a metal candleholder in the centre of the table. Do not add anything to this, for again this central unity must be uncluttered to allow for the Fire energy to move freely.

The Final Reinforcement

To really illuminate the INSPIRING energy, and to enhance and bring harmony to all your guests, place a piece of carnelian, bloodstone or red chalcedony beside your other Fire reinforcements at the far end of the room. This crystal energy will inspire and energize your fame and recognition and increase your chances for success.

A Surprise For Your Guests

Place a small offering for each guest – a tiny octagonal mirror next to each guest's place setting, wrapped in red tissue or hand-made paper. These are Fire enhancers, and will reinforce the energy which your guests carry home with them.

Food And Drink

Keep courses to a minimum for your Fire party. Fire energy is impulsive and dynamic, it needs to burn quickly or the enthusiasm will begin to fade rather than inspire. If you do want a starter and a final course, then use light, cooling foods from the selection below.

For a light starter incorporate one of the following:

Asparagus	*Prawns*
Tomatoes	*Beansprouts*
Spinach	*Mushrooms*

The main course should ideally be centred around Yang energy. Incorporate in your main course one of the following:

Onions	*Lamb*
Spices	*Red meat*
Chillies	*Smoked fish*

For a light dessert incorporate one of the following:

Strawberries	*Bananas*
Grapes	*Green tea*
Honey	*Apples*

Avoid cheese unless you really can't resist it!

Texture and colour also play a part in the Fire dinner. So try to use vibrant colours in your choice of food, as well as decoration. Dazzling colours can be found in meals like pizzas, exotic cuisine (Indian, Chinese) and showy presentation or unusual combinations of red vegetables: red cabbage, red peppers, tomatoes and aubergines all add depth of colour and culinary fire. You can also place different coloured vinegars on the table when you sit down to eat, along with hot fiery peppers in grinders, spicy pickles and mustards.

An INSPIRING dinner party needs plenty of drink to balance the generosity of fiery energy. Use sparkling wines, light white wines or champagne if you can afford it. Drink from clear or red-coloured glasses, and offer a dry martini, daiquiri or marguerita when your guests arrive. Don't indulge in sherries or beer, neither create good energy for Inspiration.

For those who prefer no alcohol, offer one of the many ranges of mineral waters, or your own fruit concoctions. Avoid lemonade, orange drinks or Coca-Cola.

THE WARMING DINNER PARTY

Setting out a dinner table for six people for a WARMING dinner party is much more informal than for Fire. The energy here is nurturing and supportive for each guest, and the main energizers radiate from the centre of the table. The element of Earth represents our home, and therefore the earth itself lies at the heart of all the other four elements.

Notice that the table in this example is round. If you have only a square or oblong table then increase the curves and softness of the dinner table with streamers, flowing muslin or ties of voile from the table legs and corners.

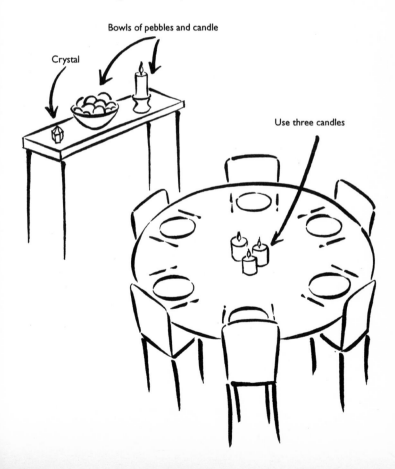

Who To invite?

Earth parties are for family get-togethers, celebrating family success, or for generally indulging with a few close friends. In this case your motives are to take the greatest pleasure with the least amount of fuss, so ensure your guests are chosen for their ease, generosity, and tolerance of others. If you do have to invite a grumpy aunt or uncle out of sheer politeness, then use the remedy below for difficult family members.

From the following animal and element signs it may be beneficial to invite one guest from each of the first two groups, and to avoid inviting those from the latter group, who may change the feel from serenity and pleasure to a more hectic mood – the last thing you want if you prefer to take your time sipping wine and savouring the puddings and sauces!

If it is too difficult to invite the specific combination of element and animal, then try to invite one of the elements listed to complement your special WARMING dinner party.

The first group will reinforce Earth energy, the second group with generate a balancer to enliven and vitalize its qualities. The last group are best avoided, as their energy is too Impatient and not suited to an Earth party.

GROUP ONE AUSPICIOUS	GROUP TWO BALANCING	GROUP THREE
Earth Dragon	Metal Snake	Wood Tiger
Earth Rabbit	Earth Horse	Wood Pig
Metal Ox	Earth Monkey	Wood Dragon
Metal Rooster	Metal Rabbit	Water Sheep
Metal Dog	Fire Dog	Water Rat
Earth Ox	Fire Ox	Water Pig

If you, your partner or close family members happen to be one of the latter category, don't worry! Balance this difficult energy with the following cure: Place a piece of malachite or amber in your kitchen and hallway.

For Earth occasions it does not matter too much where your guests sit round the table, as Earth blends with all the areas of the Bagua well. But do make sure that if you are an Earth element yourself, you sit at a round table facing the entrance to the room, and that you have behind you a solid wall. The wall can be ten feet behind you as long as you have your back to it! For other element hosts:

IF YOU ARE FIRE sit in the seat nearest the window.

IF YOU ARE METAL sit in the seat to the right of the entrance.

IF YOU ARE WATER sit in the seat opposite the window.

IF YOU ARE WOOD sit in the seat to the left of the door.

You may find that you are surrounded by too many Earth guests which can overload the energy, weighting and stagnating the ch'i. If you do find an over-emphasis of Earth then simply balance it with the following cure: Balancer for Earth party – a bronze vase or stainless-steel jug or vessel filled with white flowers. Place near the window.

The Preparation

The centrepiece of your table will be highly important as the core from which Earth energy can radiate across the table.

To reinforce the Earth energy place bundles of cinnamon sticks or bunches of dried herbs tied up with raffia, and other whole spices arranged in a wooden bowl, or if fresh herbs, in small earthenware jugs or vases. If you can't get cinnamon sticks, then use cardamom pods, nutmegs, or even a bowl of walnuts and figs on a stone or earthenware dish, placed in the centre of your table. Beside the arrangement stand three candles in metal (either chrome, aluminium, pewter or silver) candlesticks. Choose candles that are preferably yellow or soft brown autumnal colours.

Use a checked tablecloth, either yellows or reds, or plain dusky apricot, peach or ochre yellow. However, ensure your napkins and tableware are essentially white. Use round place mats if you have them, rather then square or oblong. On a side table or mantelpiece, place a bowl of pebbles or stones, fossils or shells and light a small night-light beside them once the guests have arrived.

Other Enhancements

Next to your main entrance door, the one through which your guests will enter, hang some wooden flutes, or an unusual musical instrument.

As you are empowering your environment with so much Earth energy it is important to balance the entertaining room with Metal energy.

Beside your Earth display on the side table, place a piece of white quartz crystal or a diamond if you're lucky enough to have one! If you have a ring or piece of jewellery with a diamond, use this. Use salt and pepper sets made of chrome or some other metal on your table, and add a touch of metal with tiny silver or gold stars or glitter sprinkled over your table centrepiece.

Lighting must be subtle and tranquil for a WARMING dinner party. So choose low wattage bulbs in table lamps, rather than overhead bright lights. Soft and subdued lighting can be achieved with uplighters, and if you think you're stuck because you are eating in the kitchen (and this is one of the most vitalizing places in the home to eat) you may not have considered the use of quiet and subtle lighting distributed around your working area. You can simply rectify this when you sit down to the dinner table by placing as many candles around the kitchen as you can. Or bring in a table lamp from your sitting room and stand it on the kitchen window sill.

The Final Reinforcement

To ensure that your WARMING dinner party really is harmonious, place a large piece of smoky quartz or amethyst in your centrepiece. Crystal energy is highly energizing, and for the style of dinner party you are creating you need energy which generates serenity, wisdom and tolerance.

A Surprise For Your Guests

After you sit down to eat your meal, give each guest a simple gift to take home with them. Choose something sensual but serene like a small aromatherapy candle wrapped in fine yellow tissue paper, or ochre-coloured handmade papers twisted at each end rather than tied or Sellotaped. This means your guests will take home the energy of Earth for both themselves and for all who were there.

Food And Drink

A WARMING dinner party can be as lavish as you like, but make sure you include a selection of the foods below.

Two, three or even four different dishes for one course is a languid way to stretch the pleasure and sensual delight of earthy eating. Earth is slow, and moves with a rhythm that flows and gently warms. If you want a standard three-course meal, then avoid hot spicy foods, or take a tip from the Chinese themselves, who usually have many different foods as one course, or try out a multitude of small short courses.

Have three or four complementary delights so that guests can choose from different flavours and textures, rather than eating exactly what is put in front of them.

The menu you choose ideally incorporates one or more of the following foods, and can be either part of a spread of different dishes as suggested above, or a series of three or four courses with just one simple dish for each course.

Choose one or more from:

Pasta	Olive oil
Brown or red rice	White fish
Kidney beans	Green beans
Spinach	Olives
Tomatoes	Soy sauce

These dishes can be anything from pastas with sauces, curries or Provencal cuisine. They must include sumptuous colour combinations like tomatoes and olives, or, for example, sea bass and green beans grilled in olive oil. Any combination of foods that has a quality of solidity and earthiness will be fine. Don't try using haute cuisine and dainty fiddly dishes!

Dishes as accompaniments:

Choose one from:

Garlic	Spices
Chilli peppers	Ginger
Herbs	

and one from:

Cucumber	Lemon grass
Mung beans	Broccoli
Yoghurt	Celery

If your guests are serious gourmets, then you may need to offer a choice of puddings to complete the pleasure of eating. Choose food that has light, pure, pastel colours, like sorbets, ices and fruit dishes, to balance the heaviness and sensual richness of the other courses or dishes. For example, try an exotic fruit like kiwi fruit and raspberries drenched in champagne with a dribble of brandy.

Cheese is not considered beneficial in Chinese tradition, but if you have guests who feel happier nibbling cheese and biscuits, then offer goat's cheese or flavours you have never tried before.

A WARMING dinner party will also be harmonious with sensual drinks, like velvety red wines, delicious punches, or soft sherries and ports. Drink from clear glasses with coloured stems, and if your guests prefer not to drink alcohol, then offer jugs of fruit juices or fine green teas.

THE CRYSTAL DINNER PARTY

The CRYSTAL dinner party is essentially concerned with making choices. Sometimes we are faced with a crisis, a turning point, or a decision which requires the advice and input of friends or business associates. With the energy of a CRYSTAL dinner party, you may find that the choice becomes clearer and whatever decision is made is the right one. It ensures a successful outcome.

ONLY HAVE FIVE PEOPLE

The layout suggested shows you how to set out a CRYSTAL party for five people. This is because the imbalance of numbers is crucial for the rhythm of choice. This is one of the most difficult energies, and resonates to the element of Metal. It has to be contained without becoming too powerful and extreme, so careful balancing is needed here.

Who To Invite?

CRYSTAL parties generate great intensity of purpose, and therefore it is highly important that you neither overpower the room with too much Metal energy, nor neglect it. The guests are there to improve your (or their) chances of following through a crucial decision or to ensure success in making such a choice.

Firstly, if you are a Metal element-type yourself, it is essential that you have a combination of all the elements as guests, to establish a sense of the purist form of harmony and flow of energies. In other words, you need to invite one Wood, one Fire, one Earth and one Water guest. If this is too difficult a task, then at least try to invite more from Earth and Water, rather than from Wood and Fire.

IF YOU ARE FIRE and you can't complete the balance of five energies, then at least try to invite more from Earth and Wood, rather than Metal and Water.

IF YOU ARE EARTH, and you can't complete the balance of five energies, then try to invite more guests from Fire and Metal, rather than Water and Wood.

IF YOU ARE WATER and you can't complete the balance of five energies then try to invite more guests from Metal and Wood, rather than Fire and Earth.

FINALLY, IF YOU ARE WOOD, try to invite more guests from Fire and Water, rather than Earth and Metal.

At this particular dinner party it does not matter what the animal signs of your guests are, but it can be fun guessing!

If you have succeeded in inviting five elemental types (and it doesn't matter which sex they are) then the most beneficial placement for where they may sit is shown in the diagrams below for each host element. If you can use a round table so much the better, but even an oblong table can be accommodated for five. If you feel the missing place looks odd, then just fill it with an empty chair!

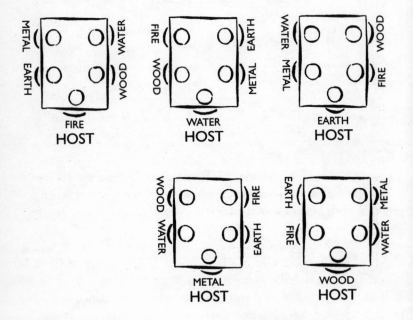

146

The Preparation

Neutrality is essential for a CRYSTAL dinner party, simply because the energy is an extremist one. Use a neutral-coloured tablecloth – soft cream, off-white or palest yellow. Don't use coloured plates, white is best, and the cutlery should be stainless steel, with simple wooden handles. Don't place napkins as they clutter up the table. However, as soon as you commence eating then it is appropriate to hand everyone a napkin, preferably white.

The centre of the table is going to contain the most powerful essence of CRYSTAL energy and for this purpose the use of white quartz crystal is highly recommended. This not only charges and receives energy, but the potent force of the crystal energy can help illuminate and give insight into the choice or future decision that has to be made.

Use a glass bowl and fill it with white quartz crystals. You can use any size of crystals and bowl, but obviously the bigger the more energized and positive the reaction. If you have any amethyst, crystal or glass paperweights you can also add these to the arrangement. Surround the bowl with a circle of tiny night-lights placed in either low candle containers or short metal candlesticks. Warning: if you do use low candle holders be careful to keep them well away from the glass as it will crack under the heat of the flames. Do not light until just before everyone enters.

NB With this party it is essential that no one sees the crystals until they enter the room. Keep them happy in the kitchen, sitting room or hallway until you're ready to eat!

Other Enhancements

In your entrance hallway or near the main door, place a single piece of amethyst to evoke clarity and honesty in those who enter your home.

To subtly balance the potent energy of Metal, you must also bring in some Earth energy. At the far end of the table (or where no one is sitting if it is a round table) place three earthenware bowls filled with black olives, green olives, pistachio nuts or red peppers. Also place here your cruet set, olive-oil drizzler and vinegar. Behind this place a glass jug of simple white flowers.

Lighting may need to be introduced to the table if there is not enough light from your centrepiece candles. Place another larger candle (perhaps a church candle) at the end of the table with your Earth enhancements.

Alternatively, use low table lamps around the room, avoid overhead ceiling lights above your crystal centrepiece. It is very important that these crystals receive and refract the light, so simply use more candles around the room if necessary.

Place a piece of obsidian on a window ledge near where you are cooking to purify the atmosphere and to give you clarity about any problems surrounding your choices.

The Final Reinforcement

Use more Metal elsewhere in the actual entertaining room, rather than having its powerful presence on the table. On a low table in the far top right area or corner of the room as you enter through the door, place a gold-, silver-, bronze- or copper-framed mirror. In front of the mirror place two small white candles in metal candleholders.

A Surprise For Your Guests

To bring harmony to your guests as well as to the occasion and to your success, give your guests a talisman suitable for each element. For each guest you can either give them one or the other of the following talismans, or for extra success, give them both.

1. Place a tiny piece of auspicious crystal beside their glass. For Water, choose from lapis lazuli or amber; for Fire, carnelian or red chalcedony; for Metal, obsidian or white quartz; for Wood, green tourmaline or malachite; and for Earth, smoky quartz or tiger's eye.

2. If you are feeling inspired and ready to activate success in other people's lives, then also place a paper 'secret' on each plate. Use a piece of handmade paper and write inside the following for each element. Use their elemental colour for the choice of paper.

   WATER — blue paper. *Secret:* do your dreams speak silently?

   FIRE — red paper. *Secret:* can you whisper wise words at dawn?

   METAL — white paper. *Secret:* shall we make music to live by?

   WOOD — green paper. *Secret:* do the winds blow gold dust?

   EARTH — yellow paper. *Secret:* is there knowing in the being?

Now carefully roll the paper up into a loose scroll and tie with raffia. Place on the correct plates according to where each guest is sitting. These are secret esoteric talismans (similar to Chinese oracles), and have a long-term beneficial effect on those who keep them safe.

Food And Drink

The CRYSTAL dinner party requires shrewd presentation of neutral foods. Courses must be neither too heavy nor too frivolous, to ensure the serious energy of the evening is contained and beneficial to your success.

Two courses are best for the CRYSTAL dinner party. The first course, to warm and nurture the guests and the environment, and the second to purify and modify the invisible energies.

For your starter, include one of the following foods in your menu. Preferably choose recipes which mean the food is totally cooked and will be served hot or warm. Choose soups and souffles, hot canapes and garlic bread fresh from the oven, rather than cold, uncooked foods like salads, crudités and pâtés.

Starter course – choose from:

Eggs	Sunflower seeds	Onions
Green peppers	Cheese	Garlic
Smoked fish		

Main Course

The second course must be simple, yet well balanced. Again, it is better to choose hot recipes, and ensure that all side dishes and extras are also 'hot' food. Incorporate one neutral food, one Yang food and one Yin food from the selection below.

Neutral – choose one from:

Chicken	Lettuce	Cauliflower
Fragrant white rice	Black-eyed beans	Carrots
Bread		

Yang food – choose one from:

Garlic	Lamb	Leeks
Potatoes	Onions	Nuts
Turkey	Hot spices	

Yin food – chose one from:

Mung beans	Mussels	Mushrooms
Clams	Prawns	Tomatoes
Crab	White fish	Soy sauce

The visual appearance of a CRYSTAL dinner party is what counts. So ensure each dish is served in either white oven dishes, stainless-steel serving plates or in dazzling chrome bowls. Use stainless-steel serving spoons and ladles. If you want to be original and are willing to try something very different, then use pewter mugs, plates and bowls.

The food also must be visually stunning, so use recipes and menus that involve the art of food presentation, to achieve a striking and impressive selection on each guest's plate. Colour and texture must be combined, so that the suggestion of complete dedication to the art of presentation has been adhered to. Use contrasting colours of food: for example, brightly coloured crabs set against the soft hues of celeriac and grated ginger, leeks baked in tomatoes and fresh basil.

Napkins are not placed on the table to begin with at a CRYSTAL dinner party, because they block the flow of energy which needs to circulate before the arrival of the guests. When you need to bring out the napkins at the start of the meal use napkin rings or holders made of brass, bronze, silver or, for pure indulgence, fake or real gold.

Glasses must be polished and have long thin stems. Dark-red-coloured glass stems are a must if you can get hold of these, as they add challenging Fire energy to stir the forces of Metal into action.

Drink can be as austere or as lavish as you like. Champagne or Vin Mousseux and sparkling wines are essential as a pre-dinner drink, as they cool and invigorate. With your meal it is not so much the type of wine, as the quality and the presence of the bottles on the table. Vision and art are crucial for the CRYSTAL dinner party to bring awareness to choices. Use beautiful bottle shapes, long necks, or labels that catch your eye, and interesting and unusual wines from fascinating places. Mineral water bottles come in a range of shapes and sizes but avoid too many different colours.

Oriental teapots and coffee makers can add a sense of sophistication to the end of the meal.

THE MAGIC DINNER PARTY

The layout for the MAGIC dinner party suggests a balance of six people. Water energy is concerned here. This enhances progress, new beginnings and can be beneficial for major career changes. It is also about the ability to communicate new ideas, so if you want to tell your friends or colleagues that you're moving abroad, or starting a new job, or just met the man or woman of your dreams then the MAGIC dinner is beneficial for enjoyment and happiness in these areas of life.

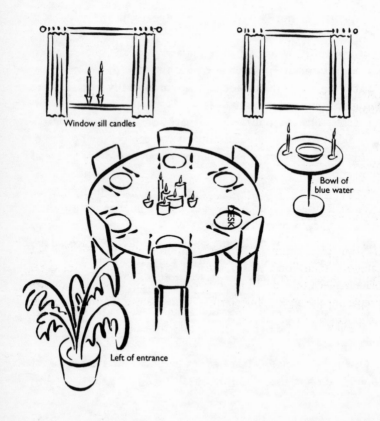

Window sill candles

Bowl of blue water

Left of entrance

Who To Invite?

Because Water energy is so flexible and changeable, the best guests to invite are those who can adapt and enjoy the unpredictability of the meal. They must be able to see that the charm of a MAGIC dinner party lies in the essence of the imagination, rather than in the actual meal. The food is just as important as at any other dinner party, but it is the guests at a Water party who are the essential ingredient, as well as the Feng Shui enhancements.

From the following groups try to invite at least one from the first group, and at least one from the second. Avoid the last group of people who may not be so harmonious with this style of party.

The first group will reinforce Water, the second group will counterbalance any excess of mood.

GROUP ONE AUSPICIOUS	GROUP TWO BENEFICIAL	GROUP THREE AVOID
Water Rat	Water Dragon	Fire Tiger
Water Snake	Metal Rat	Fire Pig
Wood Dragon	Metal Sheep	Earth Rooster
Wood Rat	Water Ox	Earth Tiger
Water Horse	Water Monkey	Fire Rooster
Wood Rabbit		

If your own animal/element combination falls in the last category, then don't worry, use the following Feng Shui cure: place a piece of sodalite in your kitchen near to where you are preparing the food. This clarifies who we are, and encourages us to let go of rigid ideas.

Depending on which element you are, here are the most auspicious locations at the table for you as host.

IF YOU ARE FIRE sit in the area of the table that corresponds to Being Cool.

IF YOU ARE EARTH sit in the area of the table that corresponds to Disclosure.

IF YOU ARE METAL sit in the area of the table that corresponds to Tolerance.

IF YOU ARE WATER sit in the area of the table that corresponds to Pleasure.

IF YOU ARE WOOD sit in the area of the table that corresponds to Flow.

If there is an emphasis on Water for this dinner party because most of your guests happen to be Water, then use some Earth energy to ground and centre the otherwise elusive energy from disappearing out of the door! Balancer for Water party: place several large stones in a group near your doorway, preferably at floor level.

The Preparation

You will see from the layout at the beginning of the section on the MAGIC dinner party that there are several Water features incorporated in the room, as well as in the centre of the table. This adds sparkle and shimmer, and makes use of the reflective qualities of Water to inspire and add to successful communication and progress.

Blue is going to play a major part of the theme, so use dark-blue or purple tablecloths, deep-coloured napkins to match, and sapphire-blue flowers in season (or fake ones). If you have any images of the sea, shipwrecks, boats, cliffs or waterfalls, then place these in your entertaining room.

For the Water features use one of the following: Place a large clear glass bowl of coloured blue water beside two blue candles and put in the area of your entertaining room on a low table near the window. The candles should be placed so that the heat does not crack the glass. Use taller glass or metal candlesticks to illuminate the water from above. If you have an indoor water fountain, then place two blue candles beside this instead.

In the centre of your table, place five deep-blue, violet or black candles in metal candlesticks (bronze effect, gold, pewter or silver, rather than stainless steel, wrought iron or chrome) and a blue glass bowl of painted shells.

Paint these shells with gold and silver pens, rich Prussian blues and violets, either all one colour or, if you are feeling creative, paint designs and motifs of stars, the moon and sun on each. Tie round each a piece of red raffia. (Ensure you have enough painted shells for the number of guests.) Use large shells, like conches and big clam shells – they are quite cheap and you can usually buy them in bags of assorted shapes and sizes.

In the centre and on top of the shells place the largest piece of amber or turquoise you can afford. Place two more deep-blue candles in front of a mirror or, if it is dark outside, a window sill, and leave the curtains open to reflect the light in the glass.

Other Enhancements

Near the entrance through which your guests will enter, place a single-stemmed flower in an opaque glass vase, either soft blue or aquamarine.

To subtly balance the generous amounts of Water energy you must also use some Wood energy. On the left side of your entertaining room on the floor as you enter, stand a large sculptural plant, with either huge upright but rounded leaves, or one that has strong branches, or unusual stems. If you don't possess any sculptural plants, then simply use cut flowers with giant leaves or blooms and stand in large earthenware or terracotta jugs.

Lighting

This must be as unusual as possible. Start with warm uplighters and table lamps. Don't light the candles until the last minute, just before the guests sit down to eat. Avoid overhead lighting for a MAGIC party.

If possible, buy some white fairy lights and adorn a huge gnarled branch, or a large bunch of unscented flowers (whatever is in season) with them. Trail the lights through the petals and leaves and place on a low table near the main dining table, for a powerful effect. Turn on only after you have lit the candles.

The Final Reinforcement

To really bring a shimmering ambience to your MAGIC dinner party, take a large, shallow glass dish, sprinkle with white petals, and place three floating candles in the centre. Place on the table nearest to you at the end of the meal, as a last unpredictable surge of energy.

A Surprise For Your Guests

The guests may not realize that the shells in the centre of the table are especially for them, so before they leave ask them to go and choose their own shell, unless you want to give them a specific one that you feel suits their nature. These are Water enhancers, and will bring good fortune and happiness with them wherever they go.

Food and Drink

A Water dinner party is essentially one where the imagination knows no bounds. However, practically speaking, the food must reflect the qualities of lightness, coolness and the tastes and aromas of the sea, rivers, lakes and water.

Choose light fish dishes – trout, sea bream, red mullet – or if you have vegetarian guests, use vegetables that are translucent: light colours like celery, lettuces, leeks, crispy seaweed or mung beans.

Two or three courses is appropriate for Water dinner parties, simply because conversation, communication and wit are at a premium. The longer one can linger over the table the better, but the food is not the most important part of the party, and it is important not to choose over-rich, indulgent, or heavy foods, which can weigh down the more fluid and elusive qualities that are needed.

For a starter course use cold foods that have either been cooked and marinated, or fresh raw vegetables: for example a melange of salads or crudites, rather than hot soups or rich cheese-based pastas. Try to include one of the following to balance the coolness of the temperature:

Radish	Onions
Black-eyed beans	Chillies
Red kidney beans	Ginger
Green peppers	

Incorporate in your main course one from the following:

Fish (River fish or sea fish, preferably unsmoked)	Crab	Almonds
	Spinach	Celery
	Tomatoes	Cabbage
Beansprouts	Beancurd	Cauliflower

For a light dessert try to incorporate one of the following:

Cherries	Raisins
Strawberries	Sugar
Peaches	Pineapple
Plums	Ice cream

The MAGIC dinner party, like any other, needs a supply of drinks, however much water energy is being activated. Use wines that are compatible with fish, like dry whites, very cold or chilled. Position buckets of ice around the room and place your bottle ready for corking. If this all sounds too cold, then finish with ports, brandies and liqueurs. If you have non-alcohol-drinking guests, then offer coffee at the end, but ensure they have a choice of jasmine tea, ice-cold tea or flavoured mineral waters.

THE DRAGON DINNER PARTY

For celebrating other people's good fortune. When our friends, colleagues or family have some good luck, financially or within their personal lives, this is the dinner party to ensure their continued success and mutual friendship and support. Sophistication is about being detached and individual, yet being aware enough to know deep down we are all just human! This dinner party offers a chance for others to celebrate their own good luck, and to benefit everyone in the future.

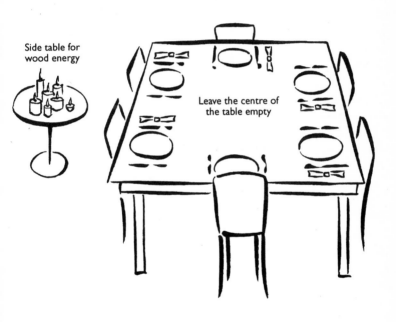

Side table for wood energy

Leave the centre of the table empty

The layout suggested above shows you how to set out a DRAGON dinner party for six people. Notice that the energizers are concentrated to the left of the table on another side table, rather than simply in the centre. This is because the potency of Wood energies can be too overpowering for the guests.

Who To Invite?

Try to avoid people who might be only interested in themselves rather than the good of the whole. From the following animal and element signs try to invite at least one from first group, and to avoid those from the second.

GROUP ONE AUSPICIOUS	GROUP TWO INAUSPICIOUS
Wood Rabbit	Metal Tiger
Wood Rat	Metal Dog
Water Snake	Metal Rooster
Water Sheep	Metal Snake
Wood Rooster	Metal Dragon
Wood Sheep	Metal Horse
Water Ox	Earth Pig
Fire Pig	Earth Ox
Fire Rooster	Earth Tiger
Fire Rabbit	
Fire Sheep	
Wood Horse	

If, however, you or your special guest is from the latter group, then use the cure suggested below.

Place a piece of verdelite (also known as green tourmaline) in the entrance hallway.

If you cannot invite any of the above auspicious guests, then try to ensure that you have at least one or two people who are Wood or Water birth elements to maximize the effect of this energy.

IF YOU ARE FIRE sit in the seat opposite the door.

IF YOU ARE EARTH sit in the seat with the door to your left.

IF YOU ARE METAL sit in any seat as long as you do not have your back to the door.

IF YOU ARE WATER sit in the seat nearest to the door.

Always make sure that if you are a Wood element yourself that you sit in the seat with the door to your right.

If you find an excess of Wood energy with too many Wood guests, then bring in some Metal energy to balance.

Balancer for Wood: A tall metal candlestick or metallic sculpture placed near the entrance to the entertaining room, either behind the door or on a side table so it is not necessarily in view on entering the room.

The Preparation

As shown in the layout above, your DRAGON energy is placed on a side table to the left of the main dinner table. Use olive greens, soft minty or aquamarine colours for tablecloths and napkins. The major theme is green dragons, so if you are able to buy or make paper dragons then place one on each place setting or attach to wooden napkin rings. You can make these paper dragons easily by copying the shape below on to green tissue or handmade paper:

Dragon design for DRAGON dinner party

In the centre of the table place four green candles in wooden holders, and surround with an arrangement of gnarled wood, dried seed pods or small sculptural plants in tiny pots. Green and brown leaf arrangements are also suitable, as are unusual spice or herb arrangements and gourds. Use wooden bowls or dishes as containers.

Other Enhancements

Next to your main front door or entrance, outside if possible, place on the left-hand side as you enter a tall green plant, shrub or flowering plant, and decorate with small green dragons cut out from handmade paper. Use the image of the dragon above, or make more stylized ones. Alternatively you can buy wooden dragons that can hang from trees, branches or plants.

To subtly balance the generous use of Wood energy you also need to bring in some Fire energy. At the end of your entertaining room, place either a red glass filled with sequins or tiny glass beads, two red candles, which should be lit only after you have lit the table candles, or hang a large mirror.

Lighting must be sophisticated. Use modern angle-poised

lights, or uplighters with reflector bulbs. Choose soft-toned bulbs, rather than harsh high-wattage or clear bulbs. Don't use pinks or reds, but try soft yellows and peach colours, or green lampshades and interesting wooden sculptures lit up from below near the light source.

The Final Reinforcement

To really enhance and bring harmony to all your guests, finally place a piece of malachite beside your group of plants and candles on the side table. This crystal energy brings empathy and relaxation, and encourages all those present to widen their compassion and enjoy other people's good fortune.

A Suprise For Your Guests

Place a small surprise gift for your guest beside each place setting. Buy the tiniest little paper gift boxes you can find (usually jewellers have these) and place inside a tiny piece of moss agate or malachite. Tie green raffia or ribbon around the box.

This Wood energy is for the well-being of all, and as such your guests will take it out into their world and their home when they leave.

Important! Don't let them open the box until they have left your premises and request that they only do so when they have arrived in their own home!

Food And Drink

The DRAGON dinner party relies on environmentally friendly food, preferably organic. This is because the energy is altruistic, and about empathy and compassion for everything in the world, not just people. DRAGON energy is supportive, so the food must also be nourishing and neutral, neither too stimulating, nor too austere.

The DRAGON menu would be best treated like a Chinese meal, where there is a first course followed by the choice of about three or four different dishes one after another, but never in huge quantities and never served together.

From the following foods choose one to be incorporated in your first course. Ensure it is organic if you can:

Starter – choose one from:

Scallops	Ham
Cheese	Red peppers
Bread	Onions
Sunflower seeds	

The next three courses can be, for example, one 'cooling' rice dish, followed by one 'heating' noodle dish, followed by different vegetables or meat dishes. Desserts are to be avoided, so it may be necessary to offer your guests a simple selection of cheeses instead.

Aroma and flavour are highly important in the DRAGON dinner party, so ensure you use recipes that use different spice combinations. Whether you opt for a variety of Indian or Chinese dishes is irrelevant: what is important is the taste.

The four DRAGON courses include one of the following 'heating' spices in each of the four courses (you can either use the same one, or a different one for each course):

Coriander	Lemon grass	Chilli powder
Black mustard seeds	Lime leaves	Cinnamon
Allspice	Ginger	Bay leaves
Garam masala	Galangal	Cardamon
Garlic		

Also include one of the following cooling foods in each of the four courses (you can either use the same one or a different one for each course).

Chicken	Egg noodles	Yoghurt
White fish	Pasta	Tomatoes
Beancurd	Mung beans	Spinach
Basmati rice	Cucumber	Mushrooms
White rice		

Drink is all about presentation for the DRAGON dinner. So find some unusual glasses or drinking vessels. If you can serve wine in stone cups, or find sophisticated glasses, or ones with green-tinted stems, then use these. Drink only white wine, which should be light, delicate and crisp, or make a point of only serving the finest green tea while the meal is in progress. Then you can resort to the more intoxicating drinks when the plates are cleared away. If you have non-alcoholic drinkers, then opt for exotic fruit mixes, or squeeze your own juice from a melange of oranges, lemons and limes topped up with soda water. As a pre-dinner drink, gin or vodka, ice cubes, a drizzle of freshly squeezed lime juice and a spot of soda water can't be beaten for awakening the taste buds.

Now you are prepared to really celebrate someone else's good fortune!

CHAPTER SEVEN

House-Warming and Welcome Parties

If you have just moved to a new home, then house-warming means exactly that. In most traditions and cultures there are ways of cleansing the energy in your new home, ridding it of old stagnant vibrations and ensuring that the environment is in harmony with you. In Feng Shui the simplest way is to use incense or purifying rituals in each room of the house, according to your own birth element. (You can look up your birth element on page 8 if you haven't already done so.)

Use one of these rituals before you begin to organize and prepare your party. They both establish your own energy patterns, and also clear negative or inharmonious energy left from past occupants.

IF YOU ARE FIRE Passion and potent energy needs to be reinforced in your home. Use the intoxicating smells of incense throughout your house. Exotic incense like sandalwood and jasmine are best to revitalize the atmosphere and drive out the negative energy. Perfumed candles or aromatherapy oils burning in a small dish are equally good, but make sure you use fragrances that are strong enough to exude throughout the house. Use a different fragrance in each room.

IF YOU ARE EARTH Centred energy needs to be reinforced. Light a white candle in your kitchen to symbolize self-respect and distinctive groundedness. Sprinkle a few pinches of ground nutmeg on the flame of the candle and then allow the fragrance to permeate the room. The rest of the house can be cleared by placing a piece of smoky quartz in the south-west-facing window or corner of your home.

IF YOU ARE METAL Purposeful energy needs to be reinforced. Take two red candles and place the first in the hallway of your home, light and then move into the main living area. Here place a piece of white quartz crystal in front of the candles while they burn for at least an hour. This both clears the house of stale or stagnant energy, and boosts your own determined style.

IF YOU ARE WATER Sensitive and imaginative energy needs to be reinforced. Place two dark-blue candles in front of a window that faces north, light them the night before and allow the reflections in the glass to dance for several hours. The rest of the house can be cleared and enhanced by placing a piece of amber near the main entrance to draw away any negative energy.

IF YOU ARE WOOD Broad-minded and sophisticated energy needs to be reinforced. Sweep the negative energy away, literally, with a broom or walk from room to room with a set of wooden wind chimes. Disperse the energy in each room by blowing gently on the chimes until they sound a few notes. Place a piece of malachite or green tourmaline in your biggest east-facing window.

Whatever your Element

If you are going to throw a house-warming party in a certain room use coloured and preferably scented candles to set the mood and clear the energy. Light them well in advance so that they have time to burn for at least twenty minutes. Here are five different mood-setters:

Red candles for dynamic fun

White candles for sophistication

Blue candles for a moody atmosphere

Green candles for informal interaction

Yellow candles for intimate friends

DISTURBING ROOMS

You might be intuitive or shrewd enough to notice difficult energy in a room. With house-warming parties especially, you may need to re-balance this room before inviting anyone into it. This is because it may still be carrying difficult forces left behind from its previous owner.

To cleanse a room, whether disturbing energy is there or not, use the following method which won't harm good energy, and will soak up the difficult energy.

Place five strands of fine gold thread (or just white cotton thread if you haven't any gold) in a small cup or bowl (this is a mixture of Metal energy for clarity and cleansing, and Earth energy for containment). Before you retire for the night prior to the party, place in the middle of the room, on the floor or on a table and leave it there overnight while you sleep. In the morning remove the bowl, take the five gold threads and plait them together or entwine them into one single woven strand before you remove it from the house. You can either place it in your outside rubbish bin, or burn it in a fire.

INVITATIONS

For house-warming parties try to make your own invites, or design them yourself. This is beneficial for you as being a new occupant in the house, to show your commitment to entertaining the house as well as your friends.

Always use your element colour in the invite somewhere, in the lettering or the paper or add a symbol or sign of which you are fond. The Chinese symbols for the elements are given below if you want to use these. A symbol for good luck and prosperity painted in hallways and entrances facing east can be very welcoming. Although we have many Western culture signs and symbols, these are a few Chinese ones which can easily be incorporated into our lives.

Element	Symbol	Colour
FIRE	火	RED
EARTH	土	YELLOW
METAL	金	SILVER
WATER	水	BLUE
WOOD	木	GREEN

If you are only working with black and white invitations, then use a symbol only. Other symbols and designs can be incorporated as borders or motifs as are the ones suggested below.

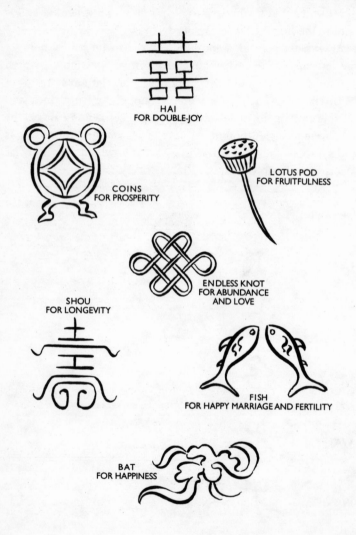

HAI
FOR DOUBLE-JOY

COINS
FOR PROSPERITY

LOTUS POD
FOR FRUITFULNESS

ENDLESS KNOT
FOR ABUNDANCE
AND LOVE

SHOU
FOR LONGEVITY

FISH
FOR HAPPY MARRIAGE AND FERTILITY

BAT
FOR HAPPINESS

THE IMPORTANCE OF A MAGIC CORNER

When you open your doors to welcome friends and warm your house, ensure there is one corner where no one can be admitted. This is a valuable place for the hidden secrets of the house to lie dormant, and also keeps both your intimate and personal security harmonious. Too many people staggering round your bedroom to look at the view, or nosey neighbours just checking out your furniture or taste, can leave behind messy energy. With a magic corner you can ensure they won't.

Choose a corner of the house where the least number of people will congregate or visit. In other words avoid the loo, kitchen, hall, or reception rooms. The bedroom could be the best place as most people are too embarrassed to spend long here, unless this is where you pile up their coats!

Alternatively be Feng Shui wise and use the space under the stairs. This is very unlikely to be visited, and if it is a cupboard and central to the heart of the house, it can be one of the most beneficial places for the house to receive the full force of this core energy.

Choose a selection of objects from the list below, one from each element, and place them in your secret corner.

FIRE MAGIC
Choose from: red candle, prism, red glass, set of small bells.

EARTH MAGIC
Choose from: smoky quartz, bowl of pebbles or shells, tapestry fabric, terracotta jug.

METAL MAGIC
Choose from: gilt-framed picture, brass rubbing, silver thread, gold-coloured cup.

WATER MAGIC
Choose from: amber, image of water (e.g. the sea), stone cup filled with coloured water, flowing fabric.

Choose from: paper sculpture, precious book, dried seed pods, wooden *objets d'art*.

Before your guests arrive visit your secret corner and acknowledge that the energy of the house here is private and contained. Although you are opening your doors and welcoming many, this is one area of your home where secrets remain.

THE GUESTS AND THE ENTRANCE

With large parties of guests there is really no need to check out everyone's element or animal sign, because usually there will be enough balance naturally. However, if you are only inviting a small number of people, say fewer than twelve, it is useful to find out if there is an imbalance in the energies. If you have invited mostly Water and Wood people, your house naturally faces south (Fire), and there are only a few Metal people, you may need to bring in some Earth energy to complement and harmonize these energies.

House-warming parties are about opening up your house for the first time and introducing new energies to the house. It is important to respect the house's own energy first and then balance the energy of the party accordingly. Below are suggestions for situations when you know the house direction and the elemental energies of your family, but you still may have many guests.

For example, you've invited twenty people, your house direction faces east, you are Wood, and your partner is Fire. Here you need to bring in Metal and Earth to balance the five energies.

Basic rule, don't let one single element dominate over all others, and if there is an element missing establish this to balance the others.

Balancing Elements

You can reinforce any missing elements with specific Feng Shui remedies. Ideally for house-warming parties these cures can be placed in the entrance hall or near the door that you welcome everyone through.

It is best to use enhancements that correspond to the warmth and welcome you are trying to create.

IF FIRE IS YOUR MISSING ELEMENT: bring in an element of rich red and gold into the reception room. Also hang a large mirror on the wall opposite the doorway. Mirrors reflect and create the dynamic energy of Fire that is always shifting and changing.

IF EARTH IS YOUR MISSING ELEMENT: bring in a plate of tempting fruits, like figs, passion fruit, apricots or pomegranates. These are all associated with the pleasures of the senses, a highly evocative energy to restore the imbalance of other elements.

IF METAL IS YOUR MISSING ELEMENT: place two single white candles in front of a mirror in metal candlesticks if you have them. If not, use kitchen foil wrapped round your candleholders for maximum effect.

IF WATER IS YOUR MISSING ELEMENT: if you have a moonstone then place it near your front doorway in a small glass bowl. Alternatively just fill a bowl with coloured water and decorate with sea shells and pebbles from the shore.

IF WOOD IS YOUR MISSING ELEMENT: use pieces of sculptured branches or old gnarled wood and place in a large terracotta pot near your main entrance. Or use images of journeys in your hallway, preferably of people or animals travelling.

THE ENTERTAINING ROOM

Because house-warming parties are usually big informal occasions you don't really have the time to balance your guests with the energy of the house apart from the method suggested above. If you are having a sit-down meal use the advice from the chapters on dinner parties and on informal suppers.

Using The Bagua

By using the Bagua you can make sure that the entertaining room is harmonized for success and enjoyment for all concerned.

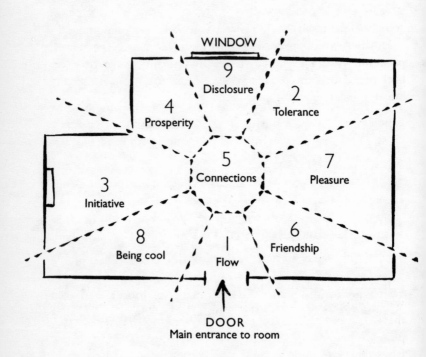

Method

Take your Bagua plan as in the diagram opposite and place it over a drawing of your entertaining room. You may have to expand or compress the plan to fit an odd-shaped room, but basically the Bagua energies will be located pretty much in the areas of the room as if it were oblong or square. Always place the Bagua with the bottom line in line with the entrance to the room as in the example opposite.

The most important area of the Bagua for big occasions, house-warming and welcome parties is the area called Friendship. Wherever in the room this area of the Bagua is located place the following Feng Shui enhancement to ensure the room is well balanced, and also use this area of the room to lay out your food or nibbles and drinks.

Enhancement: copy the Shou talisman below on to a piece of paper and place it in this area, or attach it to the wall or on the back of a door if located near one. Shou is the talisman for long life and happiness with many friends.

If you are expecting gifts as welcoming presents or house-warming presents then use the area of the Bagua in the room that corresponds to Prosperity for them to be received and placed. Obviously this area may not correspond to an easy access from the front door as most people just want to plonk their presents down as quickly as possible or push them into your hands and get to the wine. Either move a table into this area and ensure the first guests place their gifts there so everyone knows where to put them, or preferably put them there yourself.

FENG SHUI TIP

In the East bringing cut flowers and small gifts is 'not the done thing'. However, we have to remember our own Western traditions and respect our own collective customs. Always touch flowers or pot plants as soon as they appear on your table, or when they are handed to you at the door run your fingers across the petals or leaves to ensure you have welcomed them into your home.

THE KITCHEN

Unlike more intimate occasions where the energy of the guests permeates the kitchen quietly in competition with the smells of your delicious cooking, big informal parties are often filled with people coming and going, draping themselves over the sink while they eye the drinks table, or else there's a general congregation in the one room you would rather there wasn't.

To help disperse the extra hot energy in your kitchen, you may need to bring some Wood energy to balance and harmonize. This may also mean your guests circulate more and don't become kitchen wallflowers. Of course the whole purpose is a House-warming, so attaining the balance between cooling the kitchen and warming the house and your guests has to be done with subtle care and grace.

Here are a few suggestions for 'kitchen cooling' for house-warming parties:

Hang some fresh peppermint leaves from your window or on a hook near the back door.

Place a large clear glass jug filled to the brim with water and place on the window ledge; you can float some tiny glass crystals or beads on the top to add sparkling light.

Vegetables are cooling Yin foods in Feng Shui, and so a plate filled with green raw vegetables (to bring the element of Wood into the equation as well) like carrots, broccoli, cabbage, spring greens, spinach or green beans, could be placed near the cooker (but not on it!).

THE LOO

As you are trying to keep the house and your guests warm to maximize the beneficial energy of the celebration, then the loo must also have a little 'dressing'. Everyone invited to a party will probably use this room at least once, so it's important to warm and enhance this often overlooked area of the house, particularly when inviting in new friends, or when you've just moved into this new energy space.

Always remember the main Feng Shui principle to keep your loo seat closed. This prevents beneficial energy disappearing down into the waste, and can be extremely important if it is located in the Prosperity area of your house according to the Bagua. (Always see where the Prosperity area is in your house when first arriving!)

HARMONIZER – Use red or vibrant fuschia-pink-coloured soaps, sponges, pieces of coral, with stones, shells or pebbles painted gold placed in a small jar or bowl. Place on a shelf or bath, not on the loo.

COLOURS

When you've just moved into a house obviously you may hate the colour scheme, detest the carpets and choose to have your party before changing the decoration and style of your home. This is often wise – making a mess on the old worn-out surfaces won't seem so bad as wine stains on a brand new carpet.

To ensure, however, that you are creating an atmosphere which is a reflection of the warmth and hospitality you really are giving out you may have to play a few tricks with colour. If the walls are not to your own taste, there won't be a right atmosphere for a successful and prosperous beginning. Here are a few colour tips for house-warming parties:

Choose earthy colours in your decoration, i.e. warm terra-cottas, autumnal hues of ochre, burnt siennas, and desert yellows.

Outside, place old earthenware jugs or terracotta pots in a group near the front door entrance filled with yellow flowers (whatever is in season if you want real flowers, or use wonderful false flowers like mimosa or sunflowers).

The simplest way to use colour enhancement inside is with candles or with napkins and table decorations. Again, use warm colours, hues of russet and chalky reds. Try placing two candles on either side of a mirror, surround each candlestick with pomegranates, peaches and cherries, fruits that are in season, and figs, lychees or any exotic fruits from the supermarket. Use orange, cream, or ochre-coloured candles and light just before the guests arrive.

If a winter party, choose table covers and napkins decorated with warm reds and earthy rich umbers. Again, you can simply use false or real flowers in huge jugs beside the fireplace, or in the sunniest window for maximum warmth and energizing effect.

LIGHTING

The most rewarding and genuinely house-warmed parties can be attained by using soft lighting, particularly in the entrance hallway. This adds an element of diffused energy, to both warm your guests and give the welcoming area to your house a kinder light. Uplighting is a must, but if your walls don't accommodate sconces or you haven't the money or time to invest in new lighting, place candles on your hall table. Obviously these must be used with care in entrance halls and passageways, so if you can use wall candle sconces where appropriate, you will enrich and warm the walls and the deeper energies of the house itself.

In your entertaining room, again keep the lighting gentle. If this is a daytime party, let the sunlight in, but aim to provide some shade where the sun can't dazzle and overpower the warmth. The sun can be as intrusive as it is warming! Hang up some cheap muslin fabric to flow across the window and soften the glow of the mid-afternoon summer sun.

If you are having your party in the evening, again, choose warm-coloured candles, pinks, ochres, browns and soft reds, placed discriminately on the fireplace or table. Other lighting should be subdued to diffuse the energy and keep the house feeling nurtured. If you get the chance to have an open fire, use it.

FOOD AND DRINK

As house-warming parties are usually informal and either have nibbles and titbits or offer buffet-type food, indoors and outdoors, it is sensible to think only about keeping the balance between Yin (i.e. cooling foods) and Yang (heating foods). Don't worry too much about the element balance of guests for over twelve people, as usually the amount of guests and the rituals and practice you have already prepared for the occasion are all that are needed for warmth and harmony.

Choose at least THREE foods from each section to incorporate into your menu. You want to neither overheat your housewarming, nor make it too cool so that the energy becomes unwelcoming. So ensure you have a reasonable balance of both foods and as many as you like of neutral ones.

Yin (cooling) Foods

Duck	Strawberries	Cucumber
Cabbage	Grapes	Bananas
Honey	Fish	Celery
Ice cream	Apples	Spinach
Beer	Almonds	Courgettes
Oranges	Crab	Mushrooms

Yang (heating) Foods

Cheese	Smoked fish	Peanuts
Beef	Pork	Turkey
Ham	Walnuts	Sunflower seeds
Animal fat	Red peppers	Green peppers
Chocolate		

Neutral Foods

Bread	Chicken	Peas
Rice	Peaches	Pears
Pasta	Plums	

OTHER USEFUL HOUSE-WARMING ENERGIZERS

During the winter you may have the benefit of an open fire to add real warmth. Warmth, however, is also about how you feel towards others, the genuine compassion and tolerance of those with whom you want to share the magic of your new home.

Here are a few ways to improve the contentment and altruism at your party, which will benefit your home and you in the future.

CRYSTALS – Although the Chinese traditionally do not use crystal energy in their Feng Shui cures (apart from jade), Western cultures and traditions have long realized the benefit and extraordinary power of crystals in their healing and energizing properties. Their resonance is highly charged and so it is important to use the right crystal or stone for the right job. You can find these stones quite easily now in many shops. If you find it difficult to get hold of the one suggested, simply find a pebble or stone in your garden and paint it in the colours that are appropriate.

For house-warming parties use ONE of the following:

PINK OPAL – Difficult to find, but becoming more obtainable. This is a superb stone for encouraging others to lose their inhibitions. Place a small piece on your hall table, and touch it each time you pass by.

RHODOCHROSITE – A beautiful rosy-pink stone that stimulates compassion and enthusiasm for living. Great for your home to be graced with such a stone and good for activating the energy level of your house-warming party. Place in natural light on a window ledge, or if the party is at night, place beneath the glow of a candle.

ROSE QUARTZ –The most commonly available pink crystal. Use this to create a warm and loving atmosphere, and to ensure the energy of the home and the energy that is being brought in by many outsiders merges beneficially. Place centrally at the heart of the buffet table as a special decoration.

DURING THE PARTY

Energy Touching

If you feel that there are those in the room who are taking up too much energy space – they may be the types who like the sound of their own voice, or those who stand next to the buffet table and seem to have a bottomless stomach – they need to be sent invisible signals of energy to discharge their overpowering presence. You may love them, hate them, be indifferent to them, but whatever your personal feelings, you can send out an energy which touches them. You can either do this by literally touching them, i.e. putting your hand on their arm for a few seconds while you tell them an interesting or amusing story, pour them a drink or offer them some food from the oven. Alternatively, if they have resilient boundaries place your own element crystal, which may already be located in your magic corner, and resite it in the entertaining room near to where they are standing or sitting. If you notice any change in their behaviour, immediately remove the crystal, if not then leave it there as a guardian.

WHAT ABOUT YOU?

Depending on your personal birth element there are certain times of year when it is more beneficial to house-warm and welcome guests across your threshold. This is because we all resonate to certain cycles of the natural world, and although, of course, you can house-warm at any time of year, it is useful to know which is the most auspicious for well-being and long-term prosperity. (This particularly applies to people who live in temperate climates.)

FIRE – Early summer months are best, spring is lively and early autumn vitalizing. Avoid winter unless you are surrounded by log fires or fireworks to keep you warm.

EARTH – Late summer and early autumn is best; early summer is often inspiring and late autumn can be nostalgic, but avoid winter and spring or you may be yearning for everyone to leave early.

METAL – Late autumn and winter are best; early autumn can give you the motivation you need to make it a success. Avoid spring and summer, you may find yourself wanting to turn down the heat, rather than warm the place up.

WATER – Winter is your best time for informal and wild house-warming; early spring and late autumn can fill you with imaginative ideas and vision, but avoid summer or you may feel restless in everyone's company.

WOOD – Spring is your best time, but you can enjoy the freshness of early summer and the changing season of late winter. Avoid autumn and early winter when your usual tolerance and altruism may turn to impatience.

CHAPTER EIGHT

Work and Business

Depending on the reason for your business entertainment, you will have to energize yourself and your environment accordingly. This is especially important if you are trying to reach an agreement, are dealing with financial changes or crises, or having to make important investment or corporate decisions. Whatever the reason for your gathering, ensure you maximize the environment for your good first and foremost, but with regard and respect for everyone else too! You may have secret enemies, or personal issues that undermine your business relationships, but essentially, what you put out into the world will come back to you. So take care that you don't bounce a ball of negative energy into your competitor's court, or it may come back with interest!

ENERGIZING YOU AND YOUR BUSINESS/ COMPANY BEFORE THE ENTERTAINMENT

Before sitting down to do business over a meal, make sure you have energized yourself according to your elemental energy in your work environment or office. This does not have to be where you are entertaining. Often the place where we entertain for corporate lunches is a rather sterile room, a canteen, restaurant or the boardroom. There are a few tips for livening up the energy in these rooms, but for you to maximize successful dealings, attend first to your own room or office area.

Here's how:

IF YOU ARE FIRE

To improve your sense of tolerance and patience in business dealings, place a small earthenware or stoneware bowl filled with small stones, pebbles or fossils on a table, ledge or on the desk where you can see it in the area immediately in front of you. To reinforce your own qualities of inspiration, foresight and quick-thinking, place a tall-growing plant near your door and to the left of the opening. (A cactus is not really suitable unless your colleagues don't mind the sharpness of the spines!) Soft-leaved palms are best suited anyway to this interior landscape. If you don't like plants in the office hang a small round mirror on a wall in the same area. This area is your guardian energy, and you may need to take further action by ensuring no one else remains in this area for long, either standing or sitting.

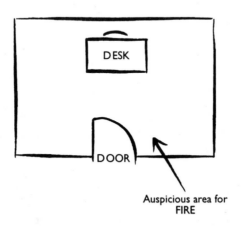

Auspicious area for
FIRE

IF YOU ARE EARTH

To improve your attitude to new directions or changes in management or company structure place a piece of carnelian or a red candle, red leather book, or even red flowers on the desk towards the top right-hand corner. To reinforce your own sense of tolerance and pragmatism, place a pile of leather-bound books, or a silk cushion on a low chair or stool, or even an antique clock or lamp on a table, in the far right-hand corner of your office. This may seem out of place in a working environment, but if you can incorporate anything old, antique or of value for its qualities of craftsmanship, then you will be ensuring that your own values and receptivity are balanced accordingly.

IF YOU ARE METAL

Improve your dealings with others by placing a small piece of rose quartz crystal on your window ledge, or on the right side of your desk. Also ensure you have on a wall behind where you sit a large black and white photographic image, or a metallic wall hanging. You can use gold or silver items on a shelf, or stainless steel, chrome or aluminium vases or *objets d'art*. Engravings or line drawings in black and white are also suitable. These bring your own energy of Metal into the environment to support and reinforce your potential. The area of the office from which you draw your strength is to your right, and is your guardian energy, so cherish it wisely and remember to keep it free from other people's energy flow.

IF YOU ARE WATER

To improve your sense of determination and to enable you to remain steadfast in your intentions, place a piece of white quartz crystal or selenite on your window ledge or on the right-hand side of the desk. To reinforce your own elemental energy for communication and tolerance of others, hang a painting, image or abstract drawing of water behind your desk. Alternatively, bring the colours blue and black into your environment, but

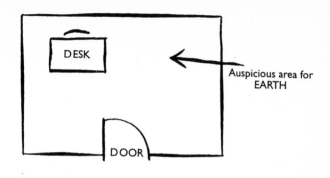

Auspicious area for
EARTH

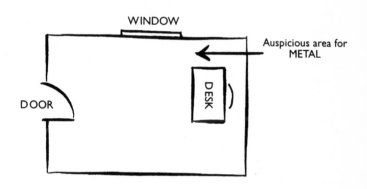

WINDOW

Auspicious area for
METAL

DOOR

DESK

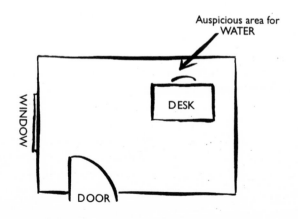

Auspicious area for
WATER

WINDOW

DESK

DOOR

make sure they are in a potent position, behind where you sit. Use inky-blue landscapes, wild sea-scapes in black frames, or model boats, ships in bottles, or a painting of shipwrecked sailors or mythological sea creatures! The area of your office which is your guardian energy is behind you, so always turn round and acknowledge this area of your room before you walk out through the door.

IF YOU ARE WOOD

To improve your ability to focus and define your objectives more clearly to others, place a world globe, chart or map of the world in the area of your office that is directly in front of where you sit, at the opposite side of the room to your desk. This may be near the door, or a window, in which case, if using a map, hang it where it is not obscured. To reinforce your own elemental energy for innovation and inspiration place a wooden box or small carved wooden bird on the left-hand side of your desk, or to the left of where you sit. This is your guardian energy area and needs to be honoured.

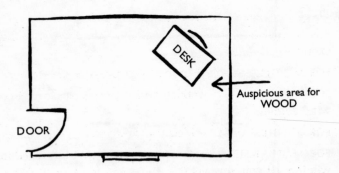

ENERGIZERS FOR DIFFERENT BUSINESS FUNCTIONS

Now you have harmonized your own office environment, you need to think about the purpose of the event. Here is a checklist of key motivations, and what energizers to bring into the room in which you are entertaining.

FOR FINANCIAL INVESTMENT OR EXPANSION – A mirror placed on a wall which does not face the door or entrance.

FOR CREATIVE INSPIRATION – An hourglass or egg-timer placed on a window ledge.

FOR PUBLIC RELATIONS – A wooden box filled with wooden beads placed on a low table.

FOR PUBLICITY AND PRESS – Red candles, or vibrant-coloured glasses.

FOR CORPORATE IDENTITY – An image from company or personal history, framed in a gold-coloured, gilt or silver frame.

FOR IN-HOUSE CELEBRATION – Change the lighting. Use soft shadows or theatrical displays.

FOR BUSINESS PLANNING – A wooden bowl filled with fruit or exotic vegetables or gourds.

FOR MERGERS – A piece of rose quartz crystal.

FOR TAKEOVERS – A wooden wind dancer, or set of wooden wind chimes.

FOR BUSINESS DEALS – Metal candlesticks, or wall sconces.

FOR MUTUAL SUCESS – A piece of yellow peridot placed in the window. (If you can't get this use yellow stones or marbles in a glass bowl.)

FOR MAXIMIZING POTENTIAL – A piece of white quartz crystal placed in a central location.

If you find that none of the above fits your purpose, then use the last key motivation – MAXIMIZING POTENTIAL – as a general all-round energizer.

Maximizing Success – A Time To Entertain

Depending on your business needs there are certain times of the day, week and year which you may find more auspicious than others to entertain.

Look at the Feng Shui Compass Wheel below to determine your favourable times.

The outer ring shows your business needs, the next circle in shows the time of day, and the inner ring the time of year.

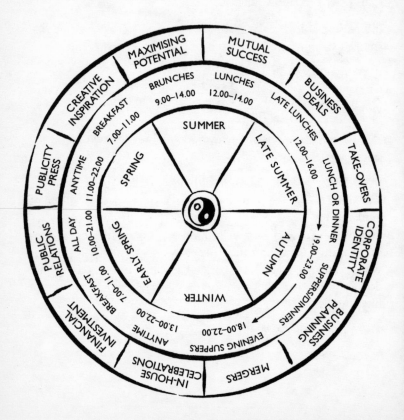

Personal Empowerment For The Shrewd Business Host

IF YOU ARE FIRE Wear something red or orange on your person. Place a good source of uplighting near your computer or on your desk, and ensure there are red cherries in your cocktails or use red glasses for your pre-lunch drinks. Women may wear an unpolished ruby, bloodstone or carnelian in their jewellery for maximum effect and to reinforce their dynamic energy.

IF YOU ARE EARTH Choose soft autumnal colours in your wardrobe – dark ochres, smoky pastels and soft yellows. Wear a piece of smoky quartz, peridot or yellow or red jasper close to your skin for determination and resilience. Bring texture into your office, with deep-piled rugs or wall tapestries, and ensure the cuisine for your entertainment includes sensual food like smoked salmon, oysters, stoned olives, and luscious fruit.

IF YOU ARE METAL Bring strong diagonals into your office – tall bamboos or fast-growing scentless lilies. Wear sophisticated non-colours – black, white, silver, pink and greys. Place a piece of white quartz on your desk, or wear diamonds if you are rich enough. If not wear any of the different kinds of garnet for joie de vivre, openness and strength of purpose.

IF YOU ARE WATER Choose rich blues, or add violets, viridians and inky blacks to your wardrobe colours. Place a piece of amber on your desk, or wear amber or turquoise on your person. Ensure you have a back-up of watery images, photos or paintings in your office like sea-scapes, mermaids, ship-wrecks, storms, waterfalls, if an aquarium is impractical. If you do have room for a tank, ensure the fish are exotic and that the filter gurgles!

IF YOU ARE WOOD Ensure that you have plenty of wood in your office apart from the furniture. Use bamboo screens, place mats or boxes. Choose natural colours like henna, ochres and olive greens in your wardrobe. Wear a piece of malachite or green tourmaline as jewellery if you are female. If a male, place a piece on your desk for poise and diplomacy.

Difficult Or Dull Entertaining Rooms
– How To Enhance And Energize For Success

The office, boardroom, penthouse suite, conference suite or whatever it's called and whatever you use, unless you are very lucky, can all seem the most dull and listless places to entertain. They are usually filled with identical chairs, office tables, boring decoration, or none at all. So if you are arranging a corporate lunch, buffet or client reception, then this is what you need to do to prepare the room and re-balance the energy.

Fire usually comes in the form of candles, or mirrors. A mirror is probably more appropriate for formal business lunches, although candles could be good atmosphere makers for early breakfast sunrisers, or evening drinks parties. Place your mirror on the wall facing the natural light source, i.e. the window. Always choose mirrors that have rounded corners. If you have access only to square or oblong mirrors make sure they have bevelled edges. The flow of energy gets locked into the hard angles of these shapes.

For Earth harmony place fresh flowers or plants at the farthest end of the room from the door. Choose plants with a strong sculptural quality, or large flowers that are not heavily scented, but add form and structure rather than prettiness – ornamental alliums, thistles, huge tropical palms, lilies.

If the room has metal and glass furniture

If the room has predominantly metal furniture don't bring any more Metal energizers into the room. Earth and Water can be incorporated freely, but use Fire and Wood with care.

Water energy can be incorporated with huge blue jugs or a set of blue inks placed on a ledge or shelf. Other energizers include hourglasses and egg-timers, or for combining traditional perspectives with innovation, an antique clock. These all represent the flow of time and are simple energizers when you may only be borrowing the room or dressing it temporarily.

Wood may already be in good supply. If not, place a pile of books on a shelf, or place a wicker rubbish basket in the east side of your room.

If the room has predominantly Wood furniture you will need to balance it with Metal.

Gold- or gilt-framed mirrors, black and white engravings or photographic images and posters are good Metal enhancers. Wrought-iron, stainless-steel, copper and aluminium sculptures, chairs or candlesticks, pen holders and vases all make excellent metal energy without being too obtrusive.

USING THE BAGUA

The Room

The following diagram shows you how to place the Bagua. (Refer to the first chapter for fuller details.) Always ensure the energy area Flow is lined up with the wall of your main entrance or doorway.

In the entertaining room you need to ensure that certain areas of the Bagua are well energized according to the occasion. The table itself will also have its own Bagua energies and the placement of certain guests can be crucial to success or failure. More details on Bagua placement with guests follows this section.

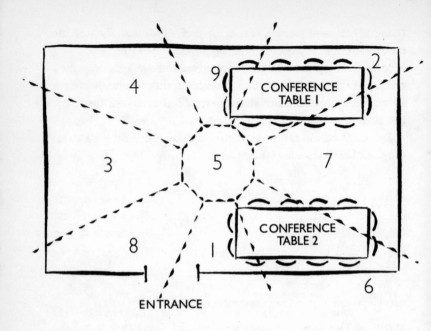

The fundamental area of your entertaining room that needs enhancement and reinforcement is the Prosperity area. The other key areas are Tolerance, Initiative, Flow and Disclosure.

Here are remedies and energizers for each of these key Bagua areas of the room:

PROSPERITY – Usually known as the money corner of your room. Energizing this space means success benefits both for you and others, rather than simply egotistic indulgence, so you must be prepared for others to prosper too!

Energizer: place a pot of money, coins, gold or silver chains, beads or jewellery in this area to increase your chances of financial and spiritual wealth. Also the use of 'money' plants, also known as 'jade' plants, are often excellent for increases in finances.

TOLERANCE – A good location of the room that focuses on reward and effort. Whatever you put into a campaign, strategy or long-term plan, if you enhance this part of the room you may well reap the benefits of hard work. But this means you have already put effort into your purpose, beliefs and your integrity, and into your relationships with others.

Energizer: best energizer is amethyst. Place a beautiful piece in this area for maximum conscious awareness.

INITIATIVE – This location of the room must be energized to ensure that others can help in your plans and schemes. Whether they are outsiders, part of the team structure or corporate ladder, or those who are vital to your financial security. You may 'advance to GO!' successfully if you ensure this part of your room is energized accordingly.

Energizer: a wooden key, wooden horse or piece of abstract carved wood. Try to use 'environmentally friendly wood'.

FLOW – This part of the room usually corresponds to the entrance, so it is important to give a good impression. The old saying 'first impressions count' is sunk deep into our psyche, so rethink it. Use this area not only to impress but to give you the feeling that liberating new ventures and deals have been given a new start and fresh chance.

Energizer: abstract art for the wall near the entrance, preferably the wall which doesn't have the door opening against it. Bronzes, marble or terracotta figures or abstract forms on a metal table.

DISCLOSURE – This area of the room will usually be opposite the doorway, and the focal point for those entering, whether a window, a wall or another door. Make sure you energize this area to enable you and your company to clarify what your objectives or accomplishments are. Important for fame, publicity and creative inspiration. For media and press coverage a good place for the drinks, buffet or pamphlets to be placed.

Energizer: use red. For example, red tablecloth, candles, books, files, strawberries, roses, red lacquer.

Other Areas Of The Bagua In The Room

The remaining areas of the room are not so potent for your business needs, unless you need promotion, patronization or financial support or are embarking on mergers, re-shuffles or staff changes. Then you need to enhance the other areas as well.

FRIENDSHIP – This area can be energized for promotional activities and affairs involving long-term strategies. For growth, production and manufacturing achievements this area is a useful one to enhance, particularly if the occasion is a lavish party or do.

Energizer: metal sculpture, or metal-framed photo or image.

PLEASURE – If you want to ensure grumpy or tight-fisted colleagues or financers relax and enjoy themselves, rather than sweat at the thought of dipping into their pockets, then use this area as an energizer.

Energizer: bamboo flutes or 'rain sticks' or other exotic musical instruments, either hung on a door, or placed on a low table.

BEING COOL – This area could be vitally important if you need to communicate without too many others becoming involved in a conflicting process. It also keeps egotism from the door, and enables others to contain and reflect, rather than be self-opinionated.

Energizer: a bowl of shells, or beautiful pebbles.

CONNECTIONS – The centre of the room is the place through which all energy flows. Therefore it is usually either free and uncluttered by people or tables, or is the central core from which all other energies radiate. If your entertaining table is central to the room, make sure you also use the following energizer on the table to ensure the unity of all the energies, and to maintain the health of the team as well as the business.

Energizer: a piece of topaz or preferably imperial topaz. If you can't get hold of this beautiful crystal, then use white quartz 'generator' crystals. These are special-shaped crystals, and you can ask for them in any shop that sells a good selection.

EXAMPLES OF CORPORATE ENTERTAINING

Here are examples of corporate entertaining rooms, the auspicious layout of the furniture and the placement or incorporation of Feng Shui enhancements.

An evening Buffet/Press reception for many

Ensure the main buffet table is at the furthest location away from the door, preferably with a window or light source behind it. Place a pair of candles in the centre, even if you don't light them, and surround them with a centrepiece of flowers, fruits or unusual gourds. Choose tablecloths in reds or yellows for zest and enthusiasm. Keep chairs away from the table and out of line

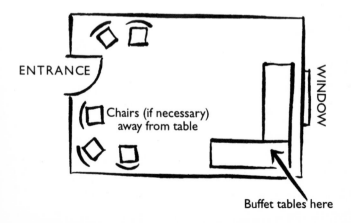

of the circling energy. Too many hard lines can mean too many hard people. If you have VIPs ensure they don't have to turn their backs to the doorway, and press photographers are best kept well away from the centre of the room to avoid conflicting energies.

A More Formal Sit-Down Lunch for Six

Ensure your most important VIPs are sitting to your left, and preferably in the seats which correspond to Initiative and/or Prosperity. Make sure that you and your important guests don't sit with your backs to the door, and that you all have a good view of the main source of light, whether the window or artificial lighting. Also ensure that you as host have your back to a wall which has a solid form placed in front of it, such as a painting, a statue, or a wall hanging. But don't sit with your back to a mirror.

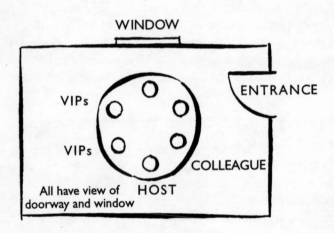

Choose tablecloths in white, soft yellows and tableware in simple stainless steel, aluminium and white. Napkins (again in white or soft pastels) and table mats can be in contrasting colours. Use as your centrepiece a red glass vase or bowl filled with unperfumed white flowers in season. Always place finger bowls with white flower heads floating on the water beside each place setting, whether you use them or not.

An Informal Brunch for Two

Keep the table as simple as possible. If it is an early breakfast, try to make sure that the sun rises to the left of you, the host, and that your guest sits opposite to you, so it will be rising on their right side. Move the table near the window if you have to ensure maximum benefit from early morning sun – even if it's obscured by clouds, it is still there. Don't ever sit with the sun rising behind you! Use vibrant colours for napkins, bowls, and plates. Fresh flowers, fruit and vegetables can be an excellent symbol of new beginnings and the morning. Choose Buck's Fizz, or just orange juice, and plenty of green China tea. Place a piece of citrine or tiger's eye on your table, and ensure the food is not placed on the table until it is ready to be eaten.

An Impromptu Sun-Downer for Four Key Guests

If you are suddenly thrown in at the deep end and have to take your important guests up to the boardroom for a few drinks at the close of the day, then make sure you place them in the most auspicious direction. If you are happy to stand and discuss business, so much the better, as then you can ensure that your important guests face the direction of the entrance. As in other placements, it is obviously important that no one stands with their backs to the door, but if someone does, let it be you!

THE BAGUA AND THE GUESTS –
WHO SITS WHERE?

Knowing something about your guests' behaviour and personality can make all the difference to whether you complete a successful deal or venture.

If you know the element and animal sign of your business guests you are off to a good start because you can use the compatibility guide on page 61 to determine how easily you are going to communicate and on what level you might expect things to be in your favour. However, if you don't know this data, depending on what you hope to achieve or implement, here is a general guide to where to place guests for maximum benefit.

Take the Bagua and place it over a plan of your table. Decide how many guests are to sit at the table and if you have eight or fewer, then you can use the Bagua easily. If you have more than eight, you may have to decide who are the VIPs and who the difficult ones. These are the people you will need to ensure sit in the most auspicious places.

As you will see in the example, the Bagua cuts the table roughly into eight areas, and has been condensed to show how easily six guests have been positioned.

Taking a Risk

Ensure that your client or guest with the biggest influence and the greatest interest in your venture is sitting in the seat which corresponds to the Initiative area of the Bagua. If the seat is located away from you being placed at the head of the table, then this is also a most honoured place for important guests. This area enhances influential energies to work for your guest, your strategy and your venture.

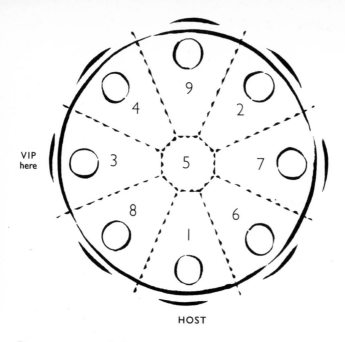

VIP here

HOST

Promoting or Selling

Whatever it is you are selling, whether your company, yourself, your product, or your ideas, place the most beneficial guest in the area of the table which corresponds to Prosperity. Your guest will derive 'good luck' in this placement, which may be of long-term benefit to you after you've completed your meal and the deal.

Buying

Shrewd judgement is necessary, particularly if it involves financial investment. So think carefully about which of your clients/guests is the most likely to tell the truth, and ensure they sit in the area of the table that corresponds to Disclosure – this is usually opposite you.

201

Negotiating

Those guests who are obviously associated with your business success can be seated in the area that corresponds to Friendship. This is where unconditional support, mutual exchange of honesty and integrity is strongly emphasized. Negotiation towards achieving the right course of action can demand you place two people in this area for maximum success. This may mean moving the chairs closer, or using a less formal arrangement then normal around the table.

DIFFICULT GUESTS

Business entertaining does not necessarily rely on friendship, and we may have to be more tolerant and compassionate about those whom we may not have chosen to sit at our table under other circumstances. Being serious about yourself, means you must also be serious about others and not judge too quickly. However, there are always some people who we just know we're not going to get on with, and those who we know won't like us much either. Here are a few stereotypes of those who may push your buttons all too easily, and where to place them. This may not turn them into saints, but it may at least bring some harmony and success to the occasion.

Egotists

These guests are often highly motivated, ambitious and some-times ruthless. Being so wrapped up in their future they may not even notice the present company. Their virtue and joy is their absolute belief in what they are doing and the conviction that they will be successful. If you want them on your side, place them at the table in the area which corresponds to Being Cool.

This is a good area to decrease selfishness and increase acceptance without diminishing any dynamism that is needed for mutual benefit.

Communicators

Not just those with excellent interpersonal skills, but those who prefer the sound of their own voice to anyone else's. These guests rarely listen to what is said to them, and are convinced they know every answer. Their virtue is they make excellent speakers, PR and promotional team players and leaders. To enhance their message rather than their vocal chords place them at the table in the area which corresponds to Tolerance. A suitable area for serenity, patience and the ability to communicate without conceit.

Hard-Liners

These guests often evoke the biggest reaction at the table. Not known for their amenable natures or willingness to give way, they are however indispensable for their shock tactics, their resolve and their record of achievement. To encourage a more open-minded and responsive approach, yet maintain their implacable loyalty, place at the table in the area which corresponds to Pleasure. This area of the Bagua is good for relaxation and flexibility without loss of integrity.

Recidivists

If you suspect others of backsliding, or double-dealing, then the business lunch may be the one place you can test out their allegiance without confrontation or obvious accusation. Place possible informers or traitors in the hot seat, in other words in the area of the Bagua known as Disclosure. Here they may reveal much more than they anticipate.

Tricksters and Machiavellis

If in doubt about one of your guest's ulterior motives, whether or not they are a conspirator or just simply out to deceive you, then place them in the Disclosure area. This area of the Bagua is excellent if you want someone to tell you their secrets! However, it may be that your suspicions are not justified and your own confidence in yourself is at a low ebb. If this is the case ensure you are seated in the area of the table which corresponds to Flow. Although most hosts choose this position through traditional expectations of being 'head of the table', it is important that you have possible manipulators directly opposite you for maximum observation, and peace of mind.

Scatterbrains

Relying on a guest who changes their mind every other sentence, or flits from deal to deal with the change in the weather without any continuity or diligence, may seem the kind of client, colleague, or investor who can't be depended on to see a future deal through. However, the joy and virtue of scatter-brains is their quick-thinking and ability to negotiate about twenty different deals at once. To ensure you get the best out of a butterfly mind place this guest in the area that corresponds to Friendship. Here they can feel comfortable in the bigger picture, and use their extraordinary wide-ranging mind without feeling trapped. This will help them to focus more on the purpose in hand.

OUT TO LUNCH –
INTERIORS NOT YOUR OWN

Now many business meetings take place out of the office. Often this is wise because it means one is instantly in neutral territory, a place where competitors, clients, deals and affairs can be sorted out in an atmosphere which doesn't give an advantage to anyone. However, to make the most of your own chances of success here are few good Feng Shui tips for entertaining out.

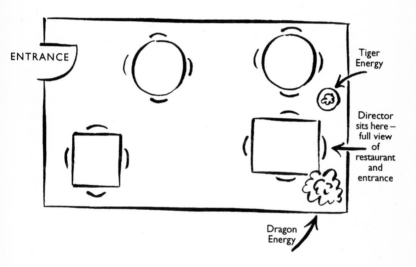

In the above diagram it is essential to follow the rule of Tortoise, Tiger, Phoenix, Dragon, for personal energy to be centred, and for maximum success to face your most auspicious direction according to your element.

In the example, this director has placed himself with a full view of the restaurant, and its entrance (Phoenix). He has a strong supporting wall (Tortoise) behind him – rather than choosing the table in the middle of the restaurant which is inauspicious for someone may be watching your back! – and the subtle, yet definitive influence of his Dragon to the left of him (a tall screen or plant), and his Tiger to the right of him (a low table or an empty chair). Obviously in a restaurant you may not have the opportunity of sitting next to a tall plant or screen or another divided area. If this is the case carry with you a small piece of white quartz crystal as a symbol of Tiger energy. Place in your left-hand pocket, or beside your plate for maximum reinforcement.

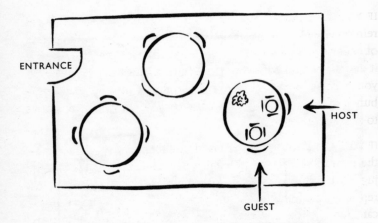

In the above diagram the guest is not sitting directly opposite, but to the left of the host. This increases the guest's sense of importance as the place of honour, and allows both the host to have his 'phoenix' area open in front of him, and also allows the guest the same principle. However, the host has also remembered to sit with his back to the main wall, facing the rest of the restaurant to ensure he is in control and in command.

IF YOU ARE FIRE, make sure there is a candle or lamp on the table. If not, then choose red wine and keep two glasses filled. You don't have to drink it! The most auspicious direction for Fire is south, but if you have to choose between a view of the entrance and the direction, the doorway view takes precedence.

IF YOU ARE EARTH, carry with you a pebble, polished stone, or piece of tiger's eye. Once you're sitting down at the table touch the stone in your pocket to energize it. Alternatively ask for a bowl of olives, and ensure you place the stones in a circle on your side plate. The most auspicious direction for Earth is south-west or north-east, but it is better to ensure you have a view of the door.

IF YOU ARE METAL, you will probably find plenty of Metal reinforcements on the table anyway, but take one of the pieces of cutlery, preferably a fork, and place towards the west, even if it doesn't line up with your place setting. Alternatively, take with you a small pouch containing two small metallic balls or a bunch of keys. Touch these when you sit down with your guests to activate the energy.

IF YOU ARE WATER, always make sure there is a jug of water on the restaurant table, or mineral-water bottles. Don't ever let the jug remain empty for long. If you finish your mineral water, just replace it with another bottle. You don't have to drink it. If you can, face in the direction north or south without disturbing your view of the doorway.

IF YOU ARE WOOD, ask if you can have a box of house matches, or some toothpicks for the table. You don't have to use them but this reinforces your Wood energy. The most auspicious direction for Wood is the east/west polarity. Obviously if you end up with your back to the door then let the direction that means you have more access to a view of the entrance take precedence.

CHAPTER NINE

Informal Suppers, Soirées and Parties

Informal and impromptu parties can often be the most fun, even if they are the most fraught with possible failure, because of the impulsive nature of such an occasion.

Those of us who can transform and shape-shift characters, moods, fashion and beliefs are off to a good start. However, whatever element and animal sign you are, you can still maximize the energy flow for harmony in your environment and in yourself before you let in the guests.

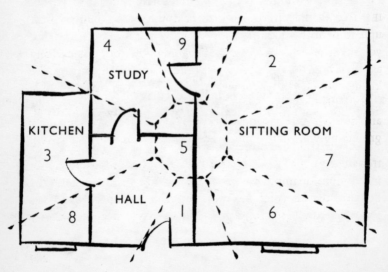

Take your Bagua map (see Chapter One on how to place and use the Bagua) and place it over a plan of your home. Whichever area or room of your house corresponds to the Bagua location Friendship, place a metal candlestick, or hang a gold-coloured or gilt-framed black and white picture, print, or photo in this room. This reinforces the beneficial Metal energy and contains and energizes the sense of support and friendship you need for an informal occasion.

Now take the Bagua map (see p. 14) and place it over a plan of the room in which you are going to entertain. This time locate the area of the room that corresponds to the Bagua energy Flow (usually the entrance to the room). Place a piece of amber near the doorway to disperse any negative energy or hang images of the sea, crashing waves, storms, serene sunsets across lagoons, anything that suggests the images of expansiveness.

ENERGIZING YOU

Some elements take easily to informality, whereas others may need extra help in overcoming their natural conventional style.

IF YOU ARE FIRE Informal occasions are a great excuse to dress up and be flamboyant. Fire loves a good audience so make sure you invite enough people or the evening will not be as exciting as you'd hoped. Take three green candles and place them on the kitchen window sill, light well in advance of your party. Sprinkle them with rosemary or thyme the day before to revitalize you and nourish your passionate nature. Wood cures are essential for grounding you yet making you feel vibrant and ready for action.

IF YOU ARE EARTH You may not be quite so eager about impromptu or impulsive get-togethers, but you may enjoy the informality of smaller and more intimate occasions. Earth likes to provide the best things in life for everyone else, so you may need to take time out to ensure you are grounded and serene. Soak in a bath filled with exotic and spicy oils and foam. Take a small round or oval mirror and hang it near the oven or cooker in your kitchen well before you start preparing the food. This brings Fire energy into the heart of your home, necessary to enhance your sense of capability.

IF YOU ARE METAL Although quite rigorous about your boundaries, you may enjoy less formal occasions just to experiment with the unknown and unpredictable. Bring red colours, vibrant paintings, or scenes of mythology, fantasy and escapism into your home. Perhaps a poster, painting or photo that might be more shocking than usual! Place a piece of carnelian in your hallway for added vibrancy, and to increase a genuine desire for passionate interaction.

IF YOU ARE WATER Informality suits you best. You may find it so relaxing that you become sucked into other people's moods too easily, which leaves you not knowing what you really and truly feel yourself. To ensure you enjoy the occasion because of who you are rather than worrying about everyone else, take a Metal wall sconce, candlesticks or an unusual metal vase, picture frame or gilt-framed mirror and place it in the room in which you are going to entertain. This will bring you integrity and trust and ensure you sparkle in true Water style.

IF YOU ARE WOOD Like Water the joys of informality are particularly suited to Wood's easy altruistic nature. However, prepare yourself for the possibility that not everyone flows to the same rhythm, and that your expectations may be higher than many other hosts. Energize yourself pre-party with classical chamber music or the gentle sound effects of the sea or flowing water. Alternatively, take a small glass bowl and fill it with water, stain it dark violet or blue to inky black and place it in the entertaining room. This will enhance your awareness of other people's feelings and ensure that the party is a success with everyone.

THE TABLE

For an informal supper party you may have an uneven number of guests. Odd numbers, or asymmetrical tables, chairs or walls, does not mean out of balance. True balance is about harmony whether chaotic or ordered. The art is to incorporate both.

With odd numbers of guests, bring in an even feel to the atmosphere with a warm-coloured tablecloth – oranges, reds, golden yellows.

Use napkins in a contrasting colour, but if you can, use glasses and plates that are different, rather than a complete matching set. This helps to energize the uneven number of guests without detracting from the flow of energy.

At a square table ensure your odd number of guests are seated like this:

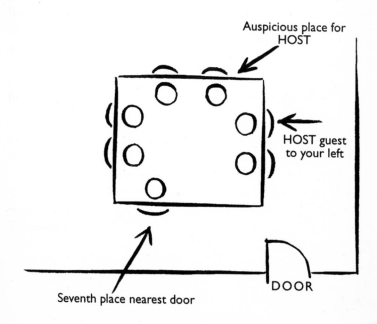

Auspicious place for HOST

HOST guest to your left

Seventh place nearest door

DOOR

At a round table it's easier like this:

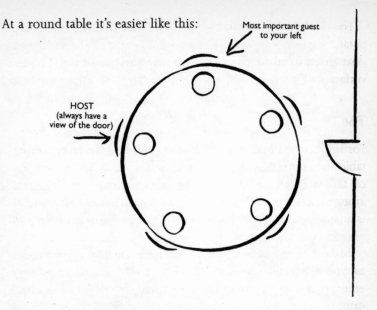

Most important guest
to your left

HOST
(always have a
view of the door)

Informal parties also mean you may have a variety of whatever is in the cupboard, or what guests bring along; this does not matter, what matters is the quality of the energy.

Use one of the following Feng Shui energizers to ensure success, whatever the menu.

For a fiery meal – i.e. chillies, Indian takeaways, Mexican food, spicy and bright-coloured dishes, place a piece of rose quartz crystal on the table as a centrepiece surrounded by a few small night-light candles.

For a cold meal – salads, lettuces, crudites, cold meats, nuts, olives, buffet-type food that you eat with fingers, place a dish of red chilli peppers or small red candles in the centre of the table. Alternatively use bright red napkins or cutlery to vitalize.

For a 'wet meal' – soups, liquid lunches, stews, casseroles, take some pieces of aluminium foil and make small silver balls. Place these in a bowl or saucer in the centre of the table, or in front of a mirror in your entertaining room.

212

For dry meals – bread, biscuits, cheese, carbohydrates, baked potatoes, place a bowl of water in the centre of the table and float your favourite rose petals or flowers in season on the surface.

The Table Layout

For buffet and finger parties, place all food in the centre of the table and ensure plates, cutlery and glasses are located on the left of the table. Put extras such as sauces, pickles, butter, oils, vinegars, cream, juices, on the right. Moving from left to right is auspicious for most guests and the general flow of energy in your room.

Make sure the table is positioned at the far top of your room as you enter the door, so that the main source of energy entering the room has a chance to circle round. This will avoid causing stagnant energy spots near the table and where your guests are receiving food.

THE ROOM

Keep the furniture from looking too set out and formal. Low sofas, cushions and a mixture of chairs and small tables are best. Avoid placing guests with their backs to the entrance, and particularly ensure that you have a vibrant supporting wall behind you as host.

If you have time to make a Feng Shui arrangement, then divide the room into two areas, one for informal talk and drinking and the other for standing and getting to know one another better. Most people prefer the standing up and chatting routine especially if they are first through the door.

Avoid encouraging people to sit down before the meal, or later on in the evening when people are beginning to leave or are waiting for that predictable garlic bread to pop out of the oven.

Stand a jug of statuesque flowers in the west area of your room. This will enhance natural altruism and genuine relaxation.

Place two table lamps on low tables or uplighters either side of the entrance or doorway, so that the light is literally showing you the way in and out to encourage *joie de vivre* and journeys.

In the east area of your room simply light a white candle, and place in front of a mirror or window to refract and inflate the energy to expand everyone's comfort zone to include themselves.

In the south area of your room place a plant which has soft rounded leaves, but does not hang down or trail. This will animate flexibility and ensure all the guests are charming.

Colour

Tranquil colours are best for informal parties, such as soft yellows, creams and the colour of old satin and pink silk. This keeps the energy tone neutral and more responsive to the different energy fields which are swirling around as your guests arrive. Place a strong bold colour, like red or orange, in the hallway to inject vivacity and sparkle into the occasion.

Use blue in the kitchen (perhaps choose a bowl of blue fruits like blueberries, plums in season or blue glass) or bring out your blue china, to enhance your sensitivity to others' needs.

Choose corn yellows, olive greens and soft ochres for table candles. Add a dash of hot pinks in your bathroom to enliven your duller guests (buy some cheap shocking-pink-coloured soaps or bath essences and line them up on the shelf or window ledge).

Lighting

Subdued is best if you haven't got to worry about the food or what you're eating. Avoid dull red lightbulbs as this will drown everyone in a glow of alien light. Mystery is best achieved by placing lights behind other objects, or candles in groups. Uplighters and free-standing lighting can enhance your favourite corners or art works of interest. Always try to have one special place you have lit up that deserves attention and admiration from your guests. It may be a favourite statue, painting or table arrangement. This reinforces your status as host. The core and the hub of the party should never be overlooked!

The Atmosphere

The habit of standing around in the kitchen, or close to the drinks table all evening, can be a little irritating for the host. First, it means that the entertaining room, beautifully lit, fine food set out, lavish decor, attention to comfort and the right music is left totally empty! To encourage your guests to stand in the appropriate room so that you can get to the kitchen sink and the fridge requires some common sense and some Feng Shui know-how.

A simple but remarkable remedy for keeping guests out of the kitchen is to hang some gorgonzola or other smelly cheese on the back of the kitchen door. This may sound ridiculous, but not only does the smell put most people off from standing around too long, but cheese is also a Yang and heating food, and will encourage potent energy. Hopefully your guests may respond to not only the smell, but the hot energy, encouraging them to stand somewhere more pleasant!

Difficult Guests

For informal parties you don't need to worry too much about your hallway and entrance, but you may receive uninvited guests, or those who have made their decision about whether to come at the last minute.

To ensure auspicious energy and to contain the dissimilar energy of those who are not consistent, place a piece of smoky quartz or citrine in your hallway, preferably in front or near a mirror or reflective source.

Food And Drink

Because you either have little time to prepare, or the occasion is only a drinks party, then food becomes less important. However, try to incorporate at least one neutral food, one heating food and one cooling food from the selection below.

Neutral – bread, chicken, rice, milk
Cooling – cucumber, asparagus, mushrooms, tea, tomatoes
Heating – potato, cheese, ham, green peppers, red peppers

Feng Shui Energizers And Balancers

Finally, place these following enhancements in the most auspicious direction in the house for you:

IF YOU'RE FIRE – Choose the south side of the home and place a lamp or sidelight there. Make sure the base and shade is either red, yellow or green.

IF YOU'RE EARTH – Locate the south-west or north-east area of your home and place a glass paperweight, or a piece of smoky quartz crystal there with two red or white candles.

IF YOU'RE METAL – Place a metal vessel, statue or candlestick in the west or north-west area of your home. Alternatively hang metal or shell wind chimes just outside a window to ensure they are somewhere where they will actually ripple and sing in the breeze.

IF YOU'RE WATER – Use a sapphire-blue glass vase or jug in the north sector of your home. Or take a clear glass bowl and sprinkle the surface liberally with blue sequins or glitter.

IF YOU'RE WOOD — Use a small water fountain or beautiful foliage plant in the east or south-east area of your home. Make sure that the plants are not flowering and that the leaves are rounded and don't trail. 'Jade' plants (also known as 'money' plants) and other succulents are excellent here.

The art of Feng Shui only works in the belief that harmony is not only for the benefit of oneself, but for the good of everyone. When entertaining we are welcoming strangers, friends and sometimes those with whom we are not so friendly into our homes. If we can be sure that our environment, food, dinner table and our hearts are in harmony, then we can be sure of keeping everyone happy, succesful and, hopefully, wise.

After the guests are gone and you are faced with the washing up, think about the pleasure of giving and receiving beneficial energy. In ancient Chinese culture, every stranger or guest you invite into your home is auspicious for your own happiness as well as theirs. So entertain, and enjoy.